The Cross in Contexts

The Cross in Contexts

Suffering and Redemption in Palestine

MITRI RAHEB

AND

SUZANNE WATTS HENDERSON

ORBIS BOOKS

Maryknoll, New York 10545

ORBIS BOOKS
Maryknoll, New York 10545

Fathers and Brothers
MARYKNOLL™

Founded in 1970, Orbis Books endeavors to publish works that enlighten the mind, nourish the spirit, and challenge the conscience. The publishing arm of the Maryknoll Fathers and Brothers, Orbis seeks to explore the global dimensions of the Christian faith and mission, to invite dialogue with diverse cultures and religious traditions, and to serve the cause of reconciliation and peace. The books published reflect the views of their authors and do not represent the official position of the Maryknoll Society. To learn more about Maryknoll and Orbis Books, please visit our website at www.maryknollsociety.org.

Manufactured in the United States of America.
Manuscript editing and typesetting by Joan Weber Laflamme.

Library of Congress Cataloging-in-Publication Data

Names: Raheb, Mitri, author.
Title: The cross in contexts : suffering and redemption in Palestine / Mitri Raheb and Suzanne Watts Henderson.
Description: Maryknoll : Orbis Books, 2017. | Includes index.
Identifiers: LCCN 2016036220 | ISBN 9781626982291 (pbk.)
Subjects: LCSH: Jesus Christ—Crucifixion.
Classification: LCC BT450 .R155 2017 | DDC 232/.3—dc23 LC record available at https://lccn.loc.gov/2016036220

Contents

v

Introduction

An Unfolding Conversation

"AN ALMOST-AUDIBLE VOICE" (SUZANNE)

"Can you recommend any resources that explain the saving power of the cross in ways that go beyond blood atonement?" The question came from Sarah, a good friend and Presbyterian pastor serving a church in the buckle of the Bible Belt, and it was a question that planted the first seeds that led to this book. Let me explain.

For one thing, Sarah explained that many in her context think the whole point of Jesus's death was to "take the fall" for our sins so we can go to heaven when we die. It's a widely popular view in American Christianity, but for Sarah and many of her church members, this theory of substitutionary atonement is a thorn in the flesh of their faith in a loving, merciful God.

They know, of course, the Bible verses that lie behind it. Gospel writers call Jesus's death a "ransom for many" (Mark 10:45; Matt 20:28); Paul uses the term, "sacrifice of atonement" (Rom 3:25); and 1 John says God sent the son "to be the atoning sacrifice for our sins" (1 John 4:10). In many instances New Testament writers indicate that Jesus died "once for all" (Heb 9:26) to restore our tarnished relationship with God.

Yet over time these cryptic phrases have evolved into wholesale theories to explain Christ's saving death. First came the notion that we were born into "original sin," and so in essence the human condition is a problem to be solved. Then came the view that the only acceptable remedy for this congenital human defect was human blood. Later interpreters added a strong dose of retributive justice to the crucifixion, stressing that Jesus was punished for our sins. Still others identified Christ as a scapegoat whose unblemished life qualified him to serve as a perfect sacrifice. Today, many extract from this array of views a pretty simple picture of the cross: it was God's plan for our personal salvation all along.

Sarah's question, I think, came less from an outright denial of atonement theology than from an increasing unease with the popular form it takes in American Christianity today. For one thing, it serves as a "get out of jail free" card in a divine Monopoly game: simply believing in Jesus secures an eternal destiny that's unrelated to life in *this* world. This view of salvation sells well in our market-driven setting, but it personalizes and spiritualizes the cross in ways that remove it from biblical story.

On another level this view of the cross can implicitly legitimize violence as a means of setting the world right. Take the case of Mel Gibson's wildly successful film *The Passion of the Christ*. Released the year after the Second Persian Gulf War began, the movie captures in Hollywood style what Walter Wink calls the "myth of redemptive violence."[1] As Gibson himself has explained, the movie was created as an evangelistic tool to impress upon viewers the sheer violence required to secure their salvation. Church members who flocked to see this movie cannot have missed its point that violent, state-sanctioned power is the solution God intends rather than the problem Jesus's death exposes and redeems.

As popular as this American version of substitutionary atonement seems to be, Sarah's question reminds us that many Christians find it disturbing if not outright dangerous. You may

---

[1] For an instructive discussion of this myth, see Walter Wink, *Engaging the Powers: Discernment and Resistance in a World of Domination* (Minneapolis: Fortress Press, 1992).

be among them. You may know the cross lies at the heart of your faith, so you don't want to skip Good Friday altogether. You may also carry a gnawing curiosity about the cross that's not adequately addressed by formulas involving a bloodthirsty God. You may even wonder, in your honest moments, if Christ's death really saves us, and if so, what it saves us from!

As a Christian New Testament scholar, I've spent a lot of my adult life considering questions like these. That's why, I think, Sarah's message stirred in me a yearning (a calling?) to write a book that reopens the question of Christ's redemptive suffering for our place and time. But I immediately faced a gut check: What do I know about suffering, especially the particular kind of suffering Jesus endured on the cross? After all, Jesus didn't die from cancer or natural disaster or even as the tragic result of human error. Jesus died as a *victim of state-sanctioned violence used to subjugate an occupied people, in order to maintain the peace and security of the empire.* As a well-educated white American woman, I have to confess that I've benefited from this kind of violence rather than suffered under it. So while I have some thoughts to offer about the saving power of the cross in its first-century context, I'm more sheepish when it comes to its redemptive meaning for our world today.

That's where Mitri enters the conversation. Just two weeks after Sarah wrote, our Charlotte congregation hosted our friend and some of his students for a four-day celebration of Palestinian arts and culture. I'd visited Mitri in Bethlehem and seen firsthand the duress of daily life under Israeli military occupation: confiscated lands, restricted movement, children yanked out of bed and hauled off to prison in the middle of the night. I'd read several of his writings and seen, through them, deep similarities between the plight of the Palestinian people today and the story of biblical Israel, including the story of a Jew named Jesus.

But that week, as Mitri spoke in auditoriums and fellowship halls and living rooms, I heard an even more powerful story about his vision for life abundant. That vision took the form of an interfaith women's soccer team delighting in victory; it glimmered in the eyes of culinary school graduates launching new restaurants; it found its way to cyberspace, where artists who couldn't travel to market created a website that generated so many orders they strained to keep pace; and it appeared on the silver screen, where documentary film students won international acclaim for the stories of creative resistance they so artfully depicted. This, I thought that week, is what the saving power of the cross looks like.

On the last morning of Mitri's visit, I awoke with a start to an almost-audible voice: "You and Mitri are going to write a book about the cross." Somewhere deep within, I sensed that anything I had to say about the biblical text would and could fall flat on its own, without the flesh-and-blood story of cross-shaped redemption Mitri has to tell. I knew, of course, that he might tell a story that strikes readers as jarring and even disorienting. But stirred by what I can only call grace, I got up, dressed, and went to church. After worship, I greeted my friend at the sanctuary door with these words: "Mitri, I have a 'vision' that involves you. Will you add your voice to mine in a book about the cross?" I'm glad he said yes, and I think his story will help you see why he did.

"A PARADIGM FOR PALESTINIAN SUFFERING" (MITRI)

Good Friday plays an important role in the life of the church in Palestine. I remember as a child crossing the street from our house to go to the Church of the Nativity on Good Friday. Although I come from a Lutheran family, Good Friday in the Orthodox Church was something different as it presented the crucifixion as an unfolding divine tragedy. Women came to church dressed in black. A corpus was hanging on a cross in the center of the church. Flowers were brought and put around the cross while the choir was singing melancholic oriental tunes.

From there I would walk to my church, Christmas Lutheran, where a moving service would bring tears to our eyes as we sang some of the most powerful selections in our hymnal. While walking back to our home, I would hear from so many homes the voice of Fairuz, a preeminent Arab opera singer, chanting her most famous songs about the crucified. So I grew up with an emotional bond to the cross, with atonement as a central part of it.

In the 1980s, during my years of study in Germany, I was exposed to a different approach to the cross: more rational, dialectic, and reflective. There I was for the first time introduced to the problematic side of atonement by studying writings of German theologians like Albrecht Ritschl, Rudolf Bultmann, Dorothee Sölle, Karl Barth, Eberhard Juengel, Jürgen Moltmann, and Wilfried Joest, in addition to non-Germans such as Japanese theologian Kazo Kitamori. As a student in Protestant theology in a German Lutheran context, I found these different writers to offer enriching, challenging, and simulating ideas that deepened my theology of the cross.

In May 1987, I finished writing my doctoral dissertation and went back to Bethlehem. I was convinced that having studied in one of the best German theological faculties, I now had answers to many difficult theological questions. However, seven months later, on December 9, 1987, the first Palestinian Intifada (Uprising) started. Clashes between Palestinian youth and Israeli military were concentrated around our church; church elders were put to prison without trial; and members of the youth group were imprisoned. Often on Sundays I had to stop preaching because the shouting just outside the church was so loud that I couldn't continue. This was a very challenging situation. I had to admit I was not prepared for something like this. I came back from Germany with lots of answers, yet no one was asking the questions for those answers.

I had to learn to listen—to listen carefully to the needs of our people; to listen to their cry; to listen to their hunger and thirst. This listening exercise took seven years. My theological studies took seven years, and listening to where people are took another seven years. I had to struggle with the question of how to preach the good news to a community that wakes up every day to more bad news. How could I speak about the cross in a context where suffering is on the daily agenda? Can the people of Palestine even *hear* a message about Christ's suffering in the midst of their own? These were the kinds of questions that kept me up at night.

In the early 1990s, during a conference on Christian-Muslim dialogue, a Muslim scholar gave a paper about the cross in modern Palestinian literature. I listened carefully and was intrigued by the number of Palestinian writers and poets, both Christians and Muslims, who wrote about the cross as a paradigm for Palestinian suffering. I started asking myself, why would Muslims write about the cross, knowing that it's an anathema in the Qur'an? Why would they use a metaphor that is not common to their readers, who are mostly Muslim? Why would they use in their writings a Christian symbol to give meaning to what's going on in their struggle? What message do they find in the cross that maybe we as Christians have missed and overlooked?

Around the turn of the century our church felt a call to start an outreach ministry with the arts as its medium for social transformation. This eventually led us, in 2006, to open Dar al-Kalima University College of Arts and Culture, the only Palestinian institution of higher education that focuses on the arts. Through this work I was exposed to the works of many Palestinian artists, both Christians and Muslims, and was again captivated to see how almost all famous Palestinian artists had at least one painting depicting the cross. From Ismael Shamout, whose painting was chosen as a cover to this book, to Nabil Anani, whose painting covers my book *Faith in the Face of Empire,* to Tayseer Barakat, Naser Soumi, Mustafa al-Hallaj, Abed Abdi, Salama Safadi, Michael Halak, Faten Anastas, and Rana Bishara, to name just few. I started asking myself, what is this power that lies in the cross that gives so much inspiration to Palestinian artists, both Christians and Muslims? What is the message in the cross that they feel is important for the Palestinian people to hear? What is it that they want to communicate through this image? Why are artists and poets so captured by the cross?

On August 9, 2008, Mahmoud Darwish, the leading Palestinian poet and artistic interpreter of the Palestinian struggle, died in Paris. His death triggered in me the desire to go back and to read all of his works in a systematic and chronological way. As I did, I was again blown away by the many biblical images, especially the cross, Darwish used in his writings through his life. Through this reading and study I realized that there is something very deep, something very existential in the cross that connects it to the struggle of our Palestinian people. There is a kind of correlation that is so profound and intense. Exploring that correlation is part of what this book is about.

"OUR PLACE AND TIME" (SUZANNE)

If we've said a bit about this book's "back story," we also want to say a word about its importance for our place and time. First, my journey in the religious studies classroom convinces me that the time is ripe for rethinking the cross and its saving power. Here's why. My students often remind me that, more than ever, the real world finds us living, working, and playing alongside people of different faith traditions—or none at all. Some find this contact so threatening they avoid all conversation about religion. But it's been my deep privilege to guide students toward meaningful religious discussions *across difference*. What they discover is that, by learning about *others'* beliefs and practices, they think more carefully about their *own*.[2] For

---

[2] A highly readable autobiography by Interfaith Youth Core founder Eboo Patel makes just this point. See his *Acts of Faith: The Story of an American Muslim, in the Struggle for the Soul of a Generation* (Boston: Beacon Press, 2007). For a similar Christian story, see Diana Eck, *Encountering God: A Spiritual Journey from Bozeman to Banaras* (Boston: Beacon Press, 1993).

my Christian students this leads quite inevitably to questions about the cross—*the* defining symbol of their faith—that they otherwise would not have considered.

Outside the classroom, too, our post-Christian context means we're facing more honestly than ever some of the harder questions about how the cross has been used as a symbol of violence and oppression for most of Christian history. From the Crusaders to the Nazis to the KKK, Christians have taken up the cross to legitimize violence in God's name. Others have used the cross to browbeat women, slaves, children, and other marginalized groups into degrading submission. But recognizing this unseemly legacy sets us free from it. For Christians, that freedom means going back to the drawing board, so to speak, back to the biblical story itself. Perhaps paradoxically, the more we learn about the cross in its first-century context, the more relevant its saving power becomes for our own place and time.

Let me put my cards on the table. As I read the news, I'm struck by a deep sense that creation is, as Paul puts it, "groaning in labor pains" (Rom 8:23), strained almost to the breaking point under the weight of death and despair. It's a global phenomenon that's pointedly local as well. From Hebron to Fallujah to Aleppo, from Ferguson to Charleston to Dallas, the cycle of violence can grow numbingly familiar.

But it's to this kind of world, in this kind of moment, that the message about the cross might yet bring a word of life. It's a word that's as personal as it is universal, as realistic as it is hopeful. As Leanne Van Dyk puts it, on the cross,

> there was some kind of victory that took place, some kind of power shift in the universe, some kind of ransom paid, some kind of healing initiated, some ultimate kind of love displayed, some kind of dramatic rescue effected.[3]

---

[3] Leanne Van Dyk, "Do Theories of Atonement Foster Abuse?" *Dialog* 35, no. 1 (Winter 1996).

In other words, though the saving power of the cross is in some ways sheer divine mystery, sheer divine gift, it's also a power that can still bring life and hope and wholeness in the most broken of places. Can Christ's death on a Roman cross two thousand years ago still save us today? Let's at least consider the possibility!

"PATTERNS THAT REPEAT THEMSELVES" (MITRI)

In many ways, this book is a "next step" in my thoughts about the cross that have continued to develop over the span of my career. Throughout these years I've struggled to connect all of these dots and to put them together. I've struggled as a Palestinian living under Israeli occupation, feeling every single day the weight of its systemic humiliation, segregation, and oppression. And I've struggled as a pastor, climbing into the pulpit each Sunday to preach the good news. In short, I've tried to make sense of our lives as Palestinians today by making sense of scripture, and vice versa.

Out of this struggle, though, I began to recognize that the ancient Israelites and modern Palestinians have much in common. I started seeing patterns that repeat themselves. I started understanding why the climax of the New Testament could not have been any other than "Jesus Christ, and him crucified" (1 Cor 2:2). After almost three decades of preaching and teaching, I captured this new perspective in my book *Faith in the Face of Empire: The Bible through Palestinian Eyes*.

Perhaps providentially, the book came out just as the Middle East was waking up to a turmoil called the Arab Spring. The Arab Spring exposed the state terror of many of the political regimes in the Middle East. At the same time it gave a push to new forms of religious terrorism that now haunt the whole region. In this context I once again saw the cross in a new light, since Jesus himself endured state terror and religious terror at the same time.

When my friend and colleague approached me with the idea of writing this book together, I said yes without hesitation. I knew that such an exercise would enrich us both. I hoped that it would give me a platform to share my story and the struggle of my people. I prayed that through this perspective coming out of the Palestinian-Christian context, people in the United States and across the globe might find a new meaning for the cross in their own lives and in the life of the world that we share.

"A FRESH AND RELEVANT AND HOPEFUL CALL" (SUZANNE)

Let me close this Introduction with a personal story. In May 2014, I led a group of college students on a trip to the Holy Land that brought to life the story of Jesus for all of us. It wasn't the holy sites so much that put flesh on the biblical account. Oh, it was almost magical to sail the Sea of Galilee, to walk the streets of Capernaum and Jerusalem, to climb the Mount of Temptation. But more than the churches or even the landscape, it was the "living stones" who made Jesus's story come to life. We listened as Christian and Muslim Palestinians detailed daily indignities of life under Israeli occupation. We heard from Jewish Israeli soldiers whose own religious tradition, they said, called them to an honest reckoning about their role in systems that degrade and subjugate. We marveled at pleas for human dignity and justice drawn by graffiti artists on the "inside" of the separation wall. We met peacemakers from all three Abrahamic faiths working creatively to foster life in their culture of death.

Near the end of our trip we shared communion on the Via Dolorosa, the path Jesus walked on the way to his death. I probably don't need to tell you what skeptics college students can be on matters of faith, and we had more than a few on the trip. But one after another, each traveler said something like this: "I get it; I see now why Jesus died. It wasn't so much to make a way for us to get to heaven. He came to bring heaven's values—God's care for all creatures—to earth."

And what happened to him? He paid a steep price. He was heckled; he came under surveillance; he was arrested; he was tortured; and he was executed. Not because he took up arms, or even a pitiful stone, against the occupation or its collaborators, but because he cast a bold vision for human flourishing in the midst of human suffering. He offered up his whole life as witness to the abundance God has in store for all of creation.

The remarkable thing is not that he died. Our world's history is full of those who have stood up to, and suffered the brunt of, evil systems of power. The remarkable thing is that his death showed the way to life—not just for his first followers, but for those today who meet the force of evil with strong acts of empowering love.

Think of the chapters that follow as an unfolding conversation. This book isn't meant to be a systematic theology; it doesn't try to pronounce, once and for all, the authoritative meaning of Christ's saving death. Above all, the cross is divine mystery, not a puzzle to be solved; amazing grace, not a concept to be mastered.

That's why we try to raise more questions than we answer, pointing out along the way some glimpses of the cross in contexts. But somewhere in this dialogue between two friends—an American professor and a Palestinian pastor—may you hear anew God's dream for the world. May you hear anew your part in it. By God's grace, may you sense deep in your marrow the saving power of the cross for your own life and for our needy world.

I

Palestine on the Crossroad, Palestine on the Cross

MITRI RAHEB

Palestine is a land at a crossroads. Historic Palestine, the land between the Jordan River to the east, the Mediterranean to the west, the Negev Desert to the south, and Mount Hermon to the north, has a unique and intriguing position in the region. The land is isolated by three natural barriers of water, deserts, and mountains. And yet the land is found at the crossroads of three continents forming a bridge and thus is anything but isolated.

Ancient maps of the Middle East, therefore, show Palestine at their center. This is the case in the mosaic map of the city of Madaba in Jordan dating from the sixth century. The map covers the area from present-day south Lebanon to Egypt, with the Old City of Jerusalem at its center. On another map Palestine is located at the center of three continents; Asia, Africa, and Europe are depicted as three leaves representing three continents held together by a center that is Jerusalem. In the Church of the Holy Sepulchre and in the middle of the Greek Orthodox church known as Catholicon, the spot is referred to

---

Excerpts from this chapter were published in Mitri Raheb, *Faith in the Face of Empire: The Bible through Palestinian Eyes* (Maryknoll, NY: Orbis Books, 2014), 49–54.

as the navel of the earth, making the point that Jerusalem is the epicenter of the world.

This might be true religiously, but politically it is nothing but a myth. Palestine is in reality a land on the cross. The land Palestine/Israel has a grand ideological reputation that does not correspond in any way to its actual size, geographic location, or geopolitical role. The media attention that Palestine receives today is in no way proportionate to its actual political standing, a disparity that is reflected in the gap between political efforts invested in "peace talks" and their (lack of) results. To understand this phenomenon, we must again look at Palestine from a geopolitical perspective.

It can be argued that Palestine is located at least geographically in the heart of the Middle East, but that does not necessarily make it the center. The opposite in fact is true. Palestine is a land at the periphery. As early as the second millennium BCE, when the five major powers of the region were emerging, Palestine did not possess the clout to join the "club of five."

From 1500 to 1200 BCE, the Near East became fully integrated as an international system that involved the entire region from western Iran to the Aegean Sea, from Anatolia to Nubia. A number of large territorial states interacted with one another as equals and rivals. Located between them, especially in the Syro-Palestinian area, was a set of smaller states that owed allegiance to their more powerful neighbors and which were often used as proxies in their competition.[1]

The prophet Ezekiel understood this well when he described Jerusalem as "in the centers of the nations, with countries all around her" (5:5). Indeed, Palestine became the place where the different magnetic fields of the regional powers would collide.

---

[1] Marc Van De Mieroop, *A History of the Ancient Near East ca. 3000–323 BC* (Malden, MA: Blackwell Publishing, 2007), 129.

The influence of the regional powers over Palestine made it into a buffer zone. Palestine was often the distance each of the empires needed from one another to feel secure or the red line that no other power should cross. In reality, and geopolitically, Palestine is, in fact, nothing but a land on the margins. Contrary to its religious reputation and geographical location, in reality and geopolitically the land lies on the periphery of the Fertile Crescent, and is a peripheral borderland for diverse empires.

Situated between different empires, the fertile plains of Palestine often became the most suitable battlefield to keep wars and their tragedies away from the heartland of those empires. Many of the regional wars between empires took place on Palestinian soil. It is no coincidence that Armageddon was envisioned as taking place in the most fertile and largest plain of Palestine. This wasn't a revealed vision of the end times, but it corresponded to the political reality of the region. Wars constitute reality in Palestine. I know this not merely from history books, but from my own experience. I am just fifty-four years old and have already lived through ten wars.

While regional powers were satisfied with Palestine as buffer zone, a buffer was not enough once a power became an empire. Empires were totalitarian in their understanding and wanted to control not just Palestine but any country in the region they could. Due to geopolitical positioning between powers, Palestine has mainly been an occupied land, occupied by the ancient and modern empires—by Egyptians, Assyrians, Babylonians, Persians, Greeks, Romans, Arabs, Crusaders, Ottomans, British, and Israelis. Sadly, it seems as if Palestine and occupation are synonymous. Historically, "Occupied Palestine" has unfortunately been the norm.

Sometimes, Palestine stood simultaneously in the sphere of influence of two regional powers; this led naturally to the land's division into two or more entities. This was the case, for example, when the Assyrians occupied the northern part of Palestine, while Egypt took control of the south. After the Assyrian occupation, two different identities developed in Palestine: one in the northern part, where the people became Samaritans; and another in the south, where the people became Judeans.

Other divisions marked successive eras. After the death of Herod the Great, the land was again divided among his sons. Something similar happened after the death of Daher El-Omar. This was true too after 1948: the State of Israel was established on 77 percent of historic Palestine, while the rest was subdivided between Jordan (West Bank), Egypt (Gaza Strip), and Syria (Golan Heights). In these cases the people of Palestine developed diverse identities, and often "neighbors" became "enemies." With no central power in place, a cycle of internal fighting erupted in the land. Against this backdrop Palestine is a land hanging between heaven and earth, between mighty regional and international powers, with little or no power at all. It is a land that is being pulled left and right, occupied, crushed, devastated, destroyed over and over again. Palestine is a land on the cross.

Not only is Palestine on the cross but so too are its inhabitants. The people of Palestine have been occupied, crushed, and oppressed by one empire after the other. It is a distinct and unique challenge to be placed in a buffer zone that's often a war zone. It is tough to see one's country as a perpetual battlefield, to see it divided and torn apart. It is enervating to feel that one's country and people are occupied not by an equal but by an empire, albeit by proxy. It is not easy to live in Palestine and survive physically and, even more, psychologically and emotionally.

But this is the context in which the people of Palestine have repeatedly found themselves. This is the context in which the Bible was written. And it is the context Palestinians face today. Throughout history, the people of Palestine have been "marked by the cross." Palestine and the cross have become synonymous. When looking for a symbol for Palestine, nothing is more powerful than the cross. The following story is a good example.

In November 2002, the Church of Sweden approached me, asking if we would have one or two paintings of Christ from a

Palestinian perspective. They were preparing an international exhibition for a Swedish audience, entitled "The Christ of the World," showing different paintings of Christ done by African, Asian, Latin American, and other international artists. The exhibition was to have its grand opening in June 2003, at the Cathedral of Uppsala, before touring different cities, galleries, and churches in Sweden. The exhibition aimed at presenting the beautiful and colorful world of the Christian Church to the Swedes and to say that the church is neither ethnic nor nationalistic, but rather crosses borders! At the same time, the exhibition was meant to offer a tool to Swedish parishes to work on their own image of Christ. Knowing that one of the missions of our center is to work on a contextual Palestinian Christian art, they approached us hoping that we could help them find and identify two such paintings.

When I received this request, I was excited because such a project fits perfectly into our mission. But at the same time, this was a challenging task. Israel had invaded Bethlehem in April 2002. Bethlehem had been under twenty-four-hour curfew for weeks, and no one knew when the curfew would be permanently lifted. What is a twenty-four-hour curfew? It means house imprisonment. No one is allowed to leave home, neither children to go to school, nor workers to go to work, nor any family member to do the shopping. Only a few hours per week is it lifted for people to address their household needs.

In this context I immediately called our art coordinator, Faten, in her home to ask for her input. We decided to meet next time the curfew was lifted for a few hours to discuss the idea in detail. A few days later, when the curfew was lifted for a few hours for people to shop for food, Faten and I met. Her suggestion was that instead of us choosing one or two paintings ourselves, we should organize a competition for all interested Palestinian artists and select the best out of their submissions. Intriguing as it was, Faten's idea raised an important question: how could we hold such a contest under curfew? Then it occurred to us that curfew indeed might be just the right time to do it. Living under curfew and house imprisonment, all of these Palestinian artists have nothing but time on their hands. Why not challenge them to use all their creativity and imagination for this task? It would help overcome their depression and anxiety, and we would have a diverse selection of paintings of Christ in the Palestinian context. In a way, the competition itself became an act of creative resistance.

Faten started working on announcing the competition. Ads were put in the most circulated Palestinian newspaper. We knew that under curfew you could not really rely on people getting the newspapers, since they were delivered only to those cities that were not under curfew. From her home Faten also contacted major art centers in the West Bank and Gaza, some by email, others by phone, since these are the only possible communication tools under curfew. December 18, 2002, was the deadline for artists to show interest by submitting a proposal, while the deadline for submitting the paintings was set for early February 2003. For almost the entire time—from November 2002 to February 2003—Bethlehem and other Palestinian towns and villages were still under twenty-four-hour curfew.

On February 6, all paintings were to be exhibited at our gallery. The gallery and the gift shop were badly damaged during the Israeli invasion of April 2002. Yet, with the help of a few organizations and churches, we'd been able to rebuild them even under the most difficult of circumstances. The exhibition "Christ in the Palestinian Context" was to be the first to be shown at the reopened gallery. When the opening of the exhibition was advertised, the announcement read "4 p.m. on February 6th if curfew is lifted on that day." By chance or by divine intervention, the curfew was lifted on that day for a few hours and the opening of the exhibition took place as scheduled. In her opening speech Faten said:

> For almost one year, it was closed and neglected. However, today, al-Kahf Gallery opens its doors once again.

In spite of all the destruction, its walls are covered with colorful paintings. Regardless of the curfew regime, it is hosting sixteen Palestinian artists coming from different places all over the West Bank: Nablus, Ramallah, Jerusalem, Bethlehem and Hebron. Some of them are well known, while others are still young beginner artists. What gathered them together was "Christ in the Palestinian Context," the topic of the exhibition. Actually, all these artists have participated in a painting competition on the same subject, overcoming by that the difficult situation and the tight closure in which they live. Each artist searched deeply in the personality and life of Jesus Christ and expressed a part of it in relation to his or her own surrounding.

When the exhibition was opened, I was on sabbatical in the United States. Only through our website was I able to have a look at the paintings. After reviewing all the paintings, I could not believe my eyes. Of all artists participating, 60 percent who submitted their paintings were Muslims. For me, this fact was not so astonishing, since over half of those who attend our programs are Muslims. Rather, I was amazed for a different reason. It was interesting to see that all of the Muslim artists, except one, had submitted a painting of the crucified Christ. Only one Christian artist had chosen this theme. (A Greek Orthodox iconographer, for example, painted a barbed wire fence preventing Jesus from entering Jerusalem, a reality we'd been living with for years.)

In the paintings I saw this message: Jesus shares our story, our history, and our destiny. Christ is very human. Christ is in solidarity with us. This is the power of the cross. In the Crucified we see ourselves; in his pain we feel our pain. In his wounds we recognize our wounds.

I could not stop thinking of the fact that the overwhelming majority of the Muslim painters chose Christ on the cross to represent the context in which they are living. We know that in the teachings of Islam, Christ was not crucified. For Christ to be crucified means nothing other than for God to be on the losing end, and that is impossible in Islam. God is greater than being a loser. We can say with Paul that for Muslims the message of the cross is nothing but foolishness. So why did these Muslim artists paint Christ, the crucified? I could only think of one answer. When they thought of their suffering and of the most meaningful message for them in that circumstance, they could not but think of Christ, the crucified. The only meaning and comfort they could find was to see the righteous hanging on the cross, powerless as they are. But they could see the power of that powerless Christ.

The message of the cross was for them so powerful that they were ready to risk painting the Crucified. At that moment they discovered that the message of the cross is stronger than any wisdom or religious teaching. In a God sharing their bitter destiny they find strength, comfort, and power. The message captured them. It captured their minds and imagination. It is the suffering and crucified Christ that can best speak to us, an occupied nation, in our suffering. It is he who can best tell our story to the world. Palestinian identity is best described by the cross.

2

The Cross and Political Power

The Way of Vulnerable Solidarity

SUZANNE WATTS HENDERSON

The real scandal of the gospel is this: humanity's salvation is revealed in the cross of the condemned criminal Jesus, and humanity's salvation is available only through our solidarity with the crucified people in our midst.

—JAMES CONE,
THE CROSS AND THE LYNCHING TREE

Such a small piece of land; such vital mythical and strategic importance. If this is true for Palestine in the twenty-first century, it was just as true in the first. As the highway from Europe to the African continent, Palestine was indeed at a crossroad of geopolitical power. But it was also a land on the cross. To "keep the peace" there, Rome imposed policies that frayed the economic and cultural fabric of society and a penal system that often rushed to deathly judgment. Violence in its many forms was the order of the day.

Into this land and among this people so deeply marked by a cross, Jesus of Nazareth was born. He stepped out into the rolling Galilean terrain as an agent from a different kind of "empire," as an emissary from a sovereign who engenders life, not death. And for this bold, counter-cultural vision, he died. Here's the point that's so often overlooked: Jesus died as one of countless victims of state-sanctioned violence. After all, the cross was a *political* symbol long before it was a *religious* one. And though Christians often make light of the earthly forces that conspired against him, the saving power of the cross is rooted in the imperial agenda that put Jesus at odds with Roman force. By pledging allegiance to God's coming kingdom, Jesus took a radical public stand that led to his death.

In this sense Jesus's crucifixion is not unique. The pages of history are full of people on the cross—victims of imperial violence justified as necessary tools for keeping the peace. Like Jesus, many have suffered not because they took up arms against the ruling power but because they promoted a just vision of human flourishing for all people. From the Confessing Church in Nazi Germany to the US civil rights movement to anti-apartheid groups in South Africa, those who take the side of the weak often suffer the violent throes of those who would protect the power of the strong.

On a deeper level, though, Jesus's death on a Roman cross *does* stand apart for Christians—and as we've seen, for some non-Christians as well! It's *the* decisive turning point in history, as the earth's axis shifts toward God's new world order. It's *the* game-changing moment, as salvation is revealed in the cross of the condemned criminal Jesus. How does this violent, deeply political death bring strength and comfort and power to the "crucified people in our midst"? How does it bring life into a culture of death? It is to these questions that we turn.

CRUCIFIXION IN CONTEXT

Our journey back to first-century Palestine begins with a survey of the Roman occupation and its violent strategies. Imperial policies wreaked havoc on this conquered people and their land. Such oppressive tactics, of course, led to both violent and non-violent resistance that elicited a potent Roman response. While organized insurgency brought brutal military reprisals, a penal system with the cross as its backbone functioned as a deterrent against challenging Rome and its minions. In all these ways the people of Palestine were a "people on the cross."

History books commonly name the era from 27 BCE to 180 CE the Pax Romana, or Roman Peace. For two hundred years Rome enjoyed internal stability and minimal unrest among its territories and at its borders. But as scholars now note, such "peace" for those in power often came at great price to those who lived under the empire's sway.

That sway extended, of course, to both Jesus's native Galilee and the region of Judea, with its holy city of Jerusalem. Here, the Pax Romana meant anything but peace and security for those who had lived there for centuries. What was the "great price" they paid? For one thing, the occupation was expensive. Besides the price tag of keeping "boots on the ground," Rome also had to budget for an adequate infrastructure to maintain a presence in the land. Travelers today can still see remains of aqueducts, roads, administrative sites, and even lavish villas, all vital parts of the occupation.

To cover these costs, Roman officials levied heavy taxes on native residents, most of whom lived in small villages and could barely get by on what their family farms produced. The Romans knew their subjects would avoid paying these taxes if at all possible, so they enlisted local residents to collect revenues by aggressive means. It was a free labor pool for Rome, since tax collectors' income came from adding, at their own discretion, a hefty surcharge to the bill. It's no wonder, then, that Jewish sources use the phrase "sinners and tax collectors" to assail those who did Rome's fiscal dirty work.

Besides charging the expense of the occupation to the subjugated people, Roman officials conscripted able-bodied men to construct the imperial infrastructure. Again, it was a cost-effective way to build impressive structures that solidified and glorified Roman authority. But again, the people paid the price: such forced labor left struggling households without their most productive workers.

By raising taxes and lowering productivity, then, the Roman occupation pushed many Palestinian communities to the breaking point. Families often had no choice but to mortgage their ancestral lands—taking on debt that was unheard of a generation before. Failed harvests brought foreclosure and forced dispossession of the land that was the people's livelihood and their identity and dignity. Though villages had long served as social safety nets, those nets were too strained to hold the weight of such social and economic stress.

Not surprisingly, a wide range of (mostly Jewish) Palestinians took issue with this value system that benefited the few (mostly outsiders) at the expense of the many (native inhabitants). During Jesus's lifetime the community at Qumran viewed both the Romans and the Jerusalem leadership as utterly corrupt. Ensconced in the Judean wilderness, this sectarian group resisted the first-century world order by withdrawing from mainstream society. Their Community Rule (found among the Dead Sea Scrolls) depicts their collective as an austere and pious outpost for God's coming kingdom; soon, they thought, God's angelic armies would swoop down to eliminate foreign forces and replace them with a divine, and decidedly righteous, occupation.

Others weren't content to wait for God to send the Romans on their way; they thought it was their job to launch holy war themselves. The Jewish historian Josephus, for instance, mentions several individual insurgents, as well as a whole movement he calls the "Fourth Philosophy." Throughout the first century these "zealots" sometimes stoked active rebellion designed to reclaim God's land for God's people, just as the Maccabeans had done two centuries earlier.

In each case, though, Roman power prevailed. When an uprising gained enough popular support, the empire pulled out all stops to reassert control over this strategically vital territory. One revolt started the Jewish War (66–72 CE), which brought the destruction of Jerusalem and the Temple in 70 CE. Just a few decades later a messianic figure named Bar Kokhba inspired an insurgency that proved to be a "final straw": after Rome regained its upper hand, much of the population was forced to relocate elsewhere.

But in most cases the Roman penal system dealt swiftly and effectively with those they called brigands before things got out of hand. As the lynchpin of that system, crucifixion constituted Rome's most brutal and dehumanizing form of capital punishment; indeed, many in polite Roman society refused even to speak of its use. For one thing, only those already considered expendable could be crucified. The sentence was off limits for Roman citizens, as well as for subjects of any repute in their own context. In practice, then, crucifixion underscored the stratified nature of a Roman society that categorized people by class and gender and ethnicity and assigned their value accordingly.

In addition, crucifixions took place in a public setting, often at an important crossroads. In this sense the cross worked as a billboard for imperial power and a not-so-subtle deterrent to those who might challenge it. Not only did the bloodied criminal show gruesome evidence of torture, but on the cross death came slowly and painfully, with the body slowly suffocating under its own weight. In all these ways death by crucifixion made a spectacle of the subhuman status assigned to the condemned.

But there's another facet of Roman crucifixion that sheds light on Jesus's death. As philosopher René Girard has explained, such brutal public executions often provide a "release valve" that settles a subjugated people in times of social unrest.[1]

---

[1] See René Girard, *I See Satan Fall Like Lightning*, trans. James G. Williams (Maryknoll, NY: Orbis Books, 2001).

Using this "single victim mechanism," those in power target a scapegoat who bears the brunt of the crowd's unaddressed rage. The victims in this scheme are often innocent bystanders from society's margins, but in the ritual killing they're portrayed as dangerous and even beastly. As Girard describes it, this mechanism whips normally peaceful people into a bloodthirsty frenzy so that, oddly and unknowingly, they join forces with their oppressor.

In all these ways Roman officials used the cross rather skillfully to solidify the people's subjugation and even win their support for their violent ways. As a symbol, the cross displayed Roman control over the human body in most graphic terms. Through crucifixion, rulers inspired both debilitating fear and, perhaps paradoxically, a placating sense of superiority. Reserved mostly for the "nobodies" of the social order, this particular form of execution flexed the muscles of Roman power in ways that signaled invincible strength.

JESUS AND THE KINGDOM OF GOD: AN "UNIMPERIAL EMPIRE"[2]

To see the cross as an icon for imperial power raises an important question: How did Jesus become a target for such an extreme form of capital punishment? What is it about his career that merited, in the eyes of Roman authorities, his public execution as a common criminal? If Jesus was simply a sweet sage spouting spiritual truths, his death on a Roman cross makes little historical sense. But he was more than that. Scholars agree he died under the banner "King of the Jews" (Mark 15:26; Matt 27:37; Luke 23:38; John 19:19). Though this gospel detail is deeply ironic for those convinced Jesus *was* God's anointed

---

[2] The term comes from Hans Leander's monograph *Discourses of Empire: The Gospel of Mark from a Postcolonial Perspective* (Atlanta: Society of Biblical Literature, 2013).

"king," it's also telling: Jesus was executed in part to make a mockery of his pretense to power.

Many who study Jesus's saving death focus mostly on his last week in Jerusalem. Some even see his suffering on Good Friday as a departure from his more "successful" Galilean career. But the Gospels tell a different story—one that portrays Jesus's work as preacher and miracle worker as the indispensable backdrop to his death on a Roman cross. As we'll see, the salvation that arrives in full measure at Golgotha already appears, in fits and starts, on the way there.[3]

Jesus in and around Galilee

There may be no more historically reliable facet of Jesus's story than his trademark message that *God was at work to reclaim the whole world.* In both word and deed Jesus of Nazareth met destructive forces of evil with the restorative power of God, and prevailed. Mark describes Jesus's "inaugural address" this way: "Now after John was arrested, Jesus came to Galilee, proclaiming the good news of God and saying, 'The time is fulfilled, and the kingdom of God has come near; repent and believe in the good news'" (Mark 1:14–15). But what did he mean by this phrase, the "kingdom of God"? And how would its arrival be "good news"?

Many today think of the kingdom of God in spiritual terms, often as heaven itself. But for Jesus, the term signaled that God's sovereign rule in heaven would soon occupy and renew the

---

[3] Keep in mind that these accounts were written decades after Jesus's death by biased writer/editors (the evangelists) who interpreted Jesus's story for early Christian believers. They combined historically reliable traditions with material that they changed or even created to "fit" what they took to be the gospel message. We will point out these differences when they're relevant to our discussion. But since we're interested *both* in Jesus's own story *and* in its meaning for his earliest followers, we'll include both more and less "reliable" material in our study.

whole earth. To declare God's coming kingdom was to pledge allegiance to an alternative and more enduring kind of empire. It was to look forward to the day when life would triumph over death.

To express this robust hope for a different world order, Jesus drew from the streams of Jewish tradition that formed and shaped him. As Mitri has pointed out, Jesus was not the first faithful Jew to find himself subject to foreign power; he was also not the first to stare down the evidence of political and economic oppression with a "word from the Lord" that it would all soon come to naught as divine justice took effect on earth.

How, then, did his spiritual forebears respond to similar circumstance? Two biblical texts forged in the fires of foreign rule lie in the background of Jesus's message. In parts of Isaiah written during the Exile (sixth century BCE), the prophet addresses a people deported to Babylon after Jerusalem's destruction. Into this moment of calamity and utter despair, the prophet relays God's promise of salvation:

> I have chosen you and not cast you off. . . .
> I will strengthen you, I will help you,
>   I will uphold you with my victorious right
>   hand. (Isa 41:9–10)

For Isaiah, the "good news" is just this: "Your God reigns" (Isa 52:7).

Jesus also channels images from Daniel's vision, which addressed in a veiled way the Syrian occupation of Palestine (second century BCE). This time, imperial forces imposed policies designed to erase the people's religious and cultural heritage. Like Isaiah, Daniel insists that God's heavenly power will soon replace the earthly occupation with a divinely sanctioned regime. Transported to God's throne room, the visionary watches as "one like a human being" (Dan 7:13) deposes his "beastly" predecessor, who seems intent on devouring the earth wholesale (Dan 7:23). Into a bleak and violent world, Daniel promises the "people of the holy ones" that they will soon take office in God's righteous, life-affirming dominion (see Dan 7:27).

In a similar way Jesus's promise that God's kingdom draws near supplies a "hidden transcript" that delegitimizes Roman power at its core.[4] In Luke, Jesus's first preaching assignment comes from Isaiah, where the prophet lays out God's platform for an "unimperial empire." As the Christ (literally, "anointed one"), Jesus takes his place as authorized agent of God's coming reign. Notice, though, what that reign looks like:

> The Spirit of the Lord is upon me,
>   because he has anointed me
>   to bring good news *to the poor.*
> He has set me to proclaim release *to the*
>   *captives*
>   and recovery of sight *to the blind,*
>   to let *the oppressed* go free,
> to proclaim the year of the Lord's favor.
>   (Luke 4:18–19, emphasis added; cf. Isa
>   61:1–4)

Where can God's power be seen? Put simply, it's wherever this messiah works on behalf of society's most vulnerable members. Though he surely appears as a religious figure—a Jewish prophet, rabbi, and mystic—Jesus also pledges allegiance to a different "empire," and that defining trait carries political implications that find him rushing headlong into the crosshairs of conflict.

But it's not just Jesus's *message* that sets him on a trajectory that leads to the cross; it's his *calculated resistance* to the present world order that proves dangerous indeed. As theologian Miroslav Volf puts it, "Active opposition to the kingdom of Satan . . . is therefore inseparable from the proclamation of the

---

[4] See James C. Scott, *Domination and the Arts of Resistance: Hidden Transcripts* (New Haven, CT: Yale University Press, 1992).

Kingdom of God."[5] In Jesus's story proclamation and active opposition go hand in hand.

What does that opposition look like? For one thing, it's an opposition that's both deeply spiritual and solidly political. Take, for instance, the story of active opposition in which Jesus liberates the Gerasene demoniac from thousands of evil spirits (Mark 5:1–20). Details in the passage suggest that it's more than a successful treatment of mental illness. Notice, for instance, the social implications of the man's condition: the physical force of evil in his life is so powerful that he's been exiled from his village to live in "the tombs" (Mark 5:2). More than just a social outcast, he's been consigned to death. Notice, too, how the spirits identify with state-sanctioned power, claiming the military term "Legion" (Mark 5:9) as their proper name. Jesus, then, meets their formidable and violent force with a power that restores the man to his "right mind" and to his community. In this glimpse of active opposition Jesus's spiritual power renews the man's mental, physical, and social well being.

Elsewhere, Jesus wields healing power through physical touch, often in violation of social and religious norms. Three Gospels tell of a bleeding woman who is desperate for release from her marginalized condition (Mark 4:25–34; Matt 9:20–22; Luke 8:43–48). Not only has her flow of blood left her perpetually "unclean," but it's also made her destitute, since she "spent all that she had" (Mark 5:26) on ineffective medical care. This time it is not Jesus who reaches out to *her* but the woman herself, who brazenly brushes the fringes of *his* cloak. Sensing that his power has "gone out," Jesus simply declares that her faith has "saved" her (Mark 5:30, 34, AT).[6] Once again,

---

[5] Miroslav Volf, *Exclusion and Embrace: A Theological Exploration of Identity, Otherness, and Reconciliation* (Nashville, TN: Abingdon, 1996), 293.

[6] Here and hereafter, when the author's translation (AT) is given rather than the NRSV, the changed text is in quotation marks or italics.

he serves—this time, unknowingly!—as a conduit for God's power to foster human flourishing in a culture of diminishment.

In some cases Jesus's active opposition to the kingdom of Satan is more subtle. For instance, his reputation for eating with "tax collectors and sinners" (e.g., Mark 2:15–16) defies carefully crafted social convention. In the ancient world social status was nowhere more evident than around the table; since the home was the microcosm of the empire, eating with one's "own people" was vital to preserving the patriarchy on which that empire was built. In a similar vein Jesus welcomes children, who were seen as emblems of weakness in the ancient world. Not only does Jesus tell his disciples to "let the little children come to me" (Mark 10:13–16; Matt 19:13–15; Luke 18:15–17), but he also offers a provocative vision for God's empire, which belongs "to such as these" (Mark 10:14).

As if to highlight the contrast between these "empires," Mark casts the story of Herod Antipas's banquet as a backdrop to God's miraculous provision in the wilderness (see Mark 6:14–44). On the one hand, Rome's client-ruler in Galilee invites privileged guests to a lavish feast. Acting impulsively out of jealousy, greed, and probably lust, Herod flexes imperial power by serving John the Baptist's head on a platter. By way of contrast, Jesus and his disciples host a lavish feast of a different order—one that makes a spectacle not by whimsical violence but by abundant provision. This banquet takes place not in a palace but in the wilderness; it has a guest list in the thousands, rather than an elite few; it nourishes rather than kills; and it transforms limited resources into abundance, rather than supplementing opulent wealth with human flesh. In all these ways God's imperial banquet carries forward the prophet's promise:

> Lo, everyone who thirsts,
>   come to the waters;
> and you that have no money,

come, buy and eat!
Come, buy wine and milk
without money and without price. (Isa
55:1–2)

Together, these gospel glimpses of Jesus's earthly mission bring to light his loyalty to an "unimperial empire." Throughout the Gospels, Jesus promotes human dignity and flourishing, especially among those at the margins. He acts in solidarity with the vulnerable through physical presence, shared meals, and even human touch. Along the way he puts flesh on God's coming reign, which will bring final release from all forces that would bind or destroy. Already, then, the seeds of his active opposition have been sown.

Jesus in Jerusalem

As long as Jesus's theater of operations stayed in the backwater region of Galilee, this provocative rabbi faced little reprisal from Roman officials. Only when he entered Jerusalem for the Passover celebration did he meet head on the imperial machine that would destroy him. It's a fate he probably sensed palpably—not just because of divine foreknowledge, but also because he knew full well that his drumbeat message about God's coming kingdom would raise the hackles of the guardians of the status quo.

What is it about Jesus's last week in Jerusalem that led Roman authorities to register him on their first-century "watch list"? For one thing, the timing could not have been more conducive, given the symbolic significance of Passover. After all, this religious festival memorializes the Hebrew slaves' divine deliverance from oppressive Egyptian overlords (see Exod 12—13), and as a sacred drama it grew intensely poignant for the covenant people during periods of foreign oppression. In Jesus's day perhaps hundreds of thousands of pilgrims living under Roman rule flocked to Jerusalem to stoke hopes that God would again secure their salvation.

The implications of Passover were not lost on the Romans, who deemed Jerusalem a tinder box during this sacred time. To help keep order, the Roman governor left a comfortable seaside home and made his authority known in the holy city. He also bolstered the military presence there several times over. By this show of formidable force, he hoped to minimize chances that Passover's celebration of freedom would erupt into outright revolution.

Within this setting Jesus quickly became a marked man. Historians think two episodes in particular helped to pave the way to his death. First, his arrival in Jerusalem seems staged as deliberate incitement. When he travels from the Mount of Olives toward Mount Zion on a donkey, Jesus assumes the role of the messianic king that Zechariah's prophecy heralds this way:

> Lo, your king comes to you;
>   triumphant and victorious is he,
> humble and riding on a donkey,
>   on a colt, the foal of a donkey.
> He will cut off the chariot from Ephraim
>   and the war-horse from Jerusalem;
> and the battle bow shall be cut off,
>   and he shall command peace to the
>   nations;
> his dominion shall be from sea to sea,
>   and from the River to the ends of the
>   earth. (Zech 9:9–10)

As agent of God's coming kingdom, this ruler triumphs not through military might but through humble power; his aim is not subjugation of "the nations" but their "peace." Notice too that the dominion he establishes dispenses with, rather than relies on, weapons of war. It's an "unimperial empire," to be sure.

Apparently, the crowds pick up on the messianic nuances of Jesus's staged journey. They wave palm branches to honor this one who "comes in the name of the Lord"; they think his prophetic act signals the "coming kingdom of our ancestor David" (Mark 11:9–10). Pent-up frustration with the Roman occupation, of course, probably intensifies their hope that Jesus will deliver the Roman "war horse" from Jerusalem. It's a hope that fits the Passover script well, and for this reason Roman authorities and their informants likely took note.

But it was Jesus's tirade against the Temple economy that probably catalyzed political forces against him (see Mark 11:15–17; Matt 21:12–13; Luke 19:45–46; cf. John 2:13–17). In all four Gospels his rant against buying and selling comes straight from his own religious tradition: "Is it not written, 'My house will be called a house of prayer for all nations'? But you have made it a 'den of robbers'" (Mark 11:17; cf. Isa 56:7). Since Jesus targets Jewish leaders who profit from the sacrificial market system, his critique may seem religious rather than political in nature.

Yet, as we'll discuss later, the Pax Romana depended on collaboration with native leaders and their sociopolitical structures, which the Romans coopted in creative ways. As historian Richard A. Horsley puts it, "The *temple-state*, as much or more than Herodian kingship and Roman governors and garrisons, constituted the face of *Roman* rule in Judea" (emphasis added).[7] Just before Jesus's birth, Herod the Great had expanded the footprint of the Second Temple in ways that blurred lines between religious and political power. For instance, its floor plan assigned different "courtyards" to different groups and so sustained imperial strategies of stratified

---

[7] Richard A. Horsley, "Jesus and Empire," in *In the Shadow of Empire: Reclaiming the Bible as a History of Faithful Resistance*, ed. Richard A. Horsley, 75–96 (Louisville, KY: Westminster John Knox Press, 2008), 80.

separation. The Temple economy, too, mirrored the imperial economy by imposing taxes and transactional fees on those who could least afford it.

This frenzied scene challenges a structural pillar of Jewish devotion precisely because the temple-state implicitly sanctions the occupying empire. And since its sacrificial system depended on buying and selling that benefited a few at the expense of many, Jesus here acts in audacious solidarity with those most vulnerable to that system. Recalling Isaiah's expansive dream for the Temple as a "house of prayer for all peoples" (Isa 56:7), Jesus assails those who've made this sacred space a trading floor where the game is rigged against the "least of these." It's one more example of his unqualified devotion to God's coming reign and its sweeping agenda of justice and righteousness.

Later, we will return to the role religious leaders played in the events of Holy Week. For now, we reiterate that Jesus's death was, above all, a *political* execution. If Jesus's prophetic acts concerned religious leaders, it was because they saw him threatening the delicate balance of power they'd forged with Rome. Even without their help edgy authorities would not have hesitated to make an example of this potential rebel. Indeed, he presented as an ideal "single victim," in Girard's scheme: he was an outsider from a remote region; he kept company with despised classes; he even came across as a delusional madman with messianic pretensions. This so-called "King of the Jews" made a perfect "release valve" for the simmering fervor of Passover. As far as the Romans were concerned, the death of this condemned criminal served several interrelated aims. It worked as deterrent to insurgents; it pacified the crowds; and it reinscribed imperial power by pitting the oppressed people against one of their own. In the process Jesus's subversive message about God's coming kingdom suffocated under the weight of his collapsing body. Or so they thought.

THE WAY OF THE CROSS:
FROM VIOLENCE TO VULNERABLE SOLIDARITY

Somehow, though, Jesus's vision for God's unimperial empire did not expire with his last breath. Rome's fearsome icon of death soon became, for a small group of Jesus's followers, a symbol of God's redemptive, life-giving power. It's a stunning transformation that occurs not *in spite of* the humiliating cause of his death but *because of* it. For them, it was his death on a Roman cross that brought salvation to the post-resurrection world. What is it about Jesus's execution that convinced these devotees that the cross brought liberation rather than oppression, victory rather than defeat?

For one thing, the cross brought the brutality of state-sanctioned violence to light. This revelatory power is critical because, as Fleming Rutledge puts it, "The beginning of resistance is not to *explain*, but to *see*."[8] Only when we square up to forces of evil do they begin to lose hold of those in their vice grip. In John's Gospel, Jesus puts it this way: "Just as Moses lifted up the serpent in the wilderness, so must the Son of Man [literally, Son of the Human] be lifted up" (John 3:14). In the biblical story the serpent represents *both sin and restoration* (see Num 21:8–9). In the same way the cross reveals the full measure of imperial power and its remedy: Jesus dies as a free man; his death on a Roman cross shows there's a way, beyond fear, to new life.

As much as any New Testament writer, Paul contends with this paradoxical notion that such a disgraceful death could usher in deliverance from evil's violent force. As a sophisticated, cosmopolitan Jew, Paul knows full well that Jesus's death on a Roman cross—so central to Jesus's gospel message—constitutes a "stumbling block to Jews and foolishness to Gentiles" (1 Cor 1:23). He knows that worshiping a "lord" who was

---

[8] Fleming Rutledge, *The Crucifixion: Understanding the Death of Jesus Christ* (Grand Rapids, MI: Eerdmans, 2015), 434.

crucified by imperial officials defies conventional views of power and strength.

Paul finds, though, that the cross subverts human notions of power. He puts it this way: "God chose what is weak in the world to shame the strong; God chose what is low and despised in the world, things that are not, to reduce to nothing things that are" (1 Cor 1:27–28). He sees the cross as God's great "no" to the empire's impulse to prevail through violence. And it is through Jesus's vulnerable solidarity with "what is weak in the world" that God's power is "made perfect in [his] weakness" (2 Cor 12:9). But how does Jesus's vulnerable solidarity usher in redemption for us? From what, in this sense, does the cross "save" us?

For one thing, the cross saves us from the delusion that strength lies in political power exerted coercively over other human beings. Jesus died as he lived: in vulnerable solidarity with human weakness. In life and death he exposed and subverted human systems—economic, social, political, and religious—that deploy strategies of separation, stratification, and violence. Along the way he defied a sociopolitical code that was the very "DNA" of the empire. Jesus's death "saves" us, in part, because it gives the lie to notions of peace and security that rest on violence and oppression.

But Jesus's death on a Roman cross saves us in another sense as well. As a decisive display of God's power, it liberates us from blind devotion to a culture of death as we cast our lot with another kind of occupation—one that dares to affirm human dignity and wholeness. Of course, this recalibration of loyalties can be costly, since it draws us, like Jesus himself, into conflict with those who would safeguard the present world order. But for biblical writers it's part and parcel of calling Jesus lord.

The apostle Paul was no stranger to suffering that came from his devotion to a crucified Lord. Throughout his letters he sees struggle as an imitation of Jesus's own destiny (cf. 1 Cor 11:1). But Paul never sounds as free as he does when he writes from prison to the Philippians. In his chains Paul finds not defeat but revelation and redemption:

> I want you to know, beloved, that what has happened to me has actually helped to spread the gospel, so that it has become known throughout the whole imperial guard and to everyone else that my imprisonment is for Christ; and most of the brothers and sisters, having been made confident in the Lord by my imprisonment, dare to speak the word with greater boldness and without fear. . . . I will continue to rejoice, for I know that through your prayers and the help of the Spirit of Jesus Christ this [circumstance] will turn out for my deliverance. (Phil 2:12–14, 18b–19)

Paul's captivity, he says, only broadens the impact of his message. Not only does word spread widely *among imperial officials*, but his suffering inspires fearlessness among others. Taking his cues from Christ, he insists that his suffering will prove redemptive as well: it "will turn out for salvation" (Phil 1:19). Though some think he has in mind his own release from jail, Paul elsewhere signals the wider landscape of salvation, which entails God's renewal of the whole earth. His vulnerable solidary with the weak, Paul thinks, carries forward Jesus's imperial agenda. His suffering, too, plays a vital role in God's redemption of the world.

For Paul, to call Jesus lord is to follow this way of the cross. Like both Jesus and Paul the Philippians have encountered resistance (Phil 1:28), probably for their active opposition to social and political forces of death. Yet Paul calls their struggle "the privilege not only of believing in Christ, but of suffering for him as well, since you are having the same struggle that you saw I had and now hear that I still have" (Phil 1:29–30). For Paul, the way of the cross is a way that resists, through vulnerable solidarity with the weak, any forces that would separate, subjugate, and kill. The suffering that resistance brings, he thinks, simply shows that God's empire is gaining ground.

Christ's death is also presented in 1 Peter as a pattern for his followers. The writer tells them to "rejoice insofar as you are sharing Christ's sufferings" (1 Pet 4:13). Though the letter doesn't provide details about the believers' "fiery ordeal" (1 Pet 4:12; see also 1:6–7), it does see *their* persecution as an inherent part of *Christ's* redemptive work. Scholars think their suffering is probably both social and political in nature. Remember, the cross wasn't exactly a status symbol in the Roman Empire. Besides, the "Christ cult" had gained a questionable reputation; its makeup of mixed races and classes violated social protocol. But the writer is clear: to suffer "as a Christian" is not a "disgrace" (1 Pet 4:16), because their suffering reveals God's power and glory. Like Christ's suffering, theirs exposes the contours of God's redemptive power.

Finally, the book of Revelation offers a dazzling, dramatic picture of the power play that occurs as God's occupation replaces Rome's. In this series of bizarre visions John watches as cosmic conflict gives way, in the end, to redemption and hope. Along the way those who pledge allegiance to God's reign suffer the throes of violence meted out by the (imperial) "beast": they're even "beheaded for their testimony to Jesus" because they won't worship the beast (Rev 20:4). Like Jesus, they resist imperial power by taking a stand for God's power. As a result, they become vulnerable to a culture of death. Yet, like Jesus, their death is not the end of the story, since they too will "come to life and reign with Christ" (Rev 20:4).

CONCLUDING THOUGHTS

Biblical reflection on Jesus's saving death does not shy away from the political implications of pledging allegiance to God's kingdom—either for Jesus or for his followers. The fact that Jesus died on a Roman cross should remind us that the occupation deemed him a "clear and present danger" to imperial power. To move too quickly to a personal or spiritual view of the cross is to neglect its political implications. It's also to overlook the evidence that his earliest followers saw Jesus's death less as an isolated event than as a pattern of faithful devotion to God. For them, the cross became "an example, so that you should follow in his steps" (1 Pet 2:21).

What does it look like, in our own context, to follow this example? What does it look like to stand in vulnerable solidarity with those at the margins of society, with those who suffer under political systems that promote "peace and security" by means of state-sanctioned violence? Two thousand years later these questions remain profoundly on point for a world still writhing under conventional, imperial power.

For those of us who enjoy the privilege and prosperity of that power—I count myself in this group—the call is as challenging as it is clear. Jesus invites us, as he invited his first followers, not just to *say* that God loves and values all people but to *resist* political forces at work to separate, subjugate, and even kill. For Jesus, that resistance began when he crossed social and political boundaries to stand in proximity to those at the margins.[9] He went beyond proximity, though, to take up the cause of the weak by channeling God's life-giving power. But don't miss this point: he didn't just *endorse* their concerns; his authentic solidarity with the vulnerable made *him* vulnerable as well, "even to the point of death on a cross" (Phil 2:8).

For those who count themselves among society's despised, dismissed, or devalued members, the saving power of the cross may be this: God is in your very midst, hanging with you in the darkest moments of despair and death. God neither trivializes your suffering nor endorses its perpetrators. But God does use

---

[9] On the power of proximity to redeem the criminal justice system, see Bryan Stephenson, *Just Mercy: A Story of Justice and Redemption* (New York: Random House, 2014).

it—and you—to expose true power to the world. For those who have eyes to see, you are the very face of Christ.

Here's the saving power of the cross I want to reclaim. From our post-resurrection vantage point we know that death is not the end of the story. Though the Romans *thought* they eliminated Jesus's threat to imperial power, that threat lives on, though not by conventional means. It lives on wherever we too cross social and political boundaries to stand in proximity to— and vulnerable solidarity with—people who find themselves "on the cross" today. It lives on wherever our "active opposition to the kingdom of Satan" expands the footprint of God's occupation. It lives on wherever we opt out of any political power deployed to "hurt or destroy" (Isa 11:9) and opt in as agents of God's power to bring life, even out of death itself.

3

The Cross, the State,
and Religious Terror

MITRI RAHEB

I was born in the little town of Bethlehem in 1962. At that time Bethlehem was still a little town of fewer than fifteen thousand people, most of whom were Christians. Bethlehem was still a peaceful town where everyone knew everyone. But over the years I've watched as the Israeli occupation has tightened its deathly grip on my people.

Our oppression started, though, long before I was born, and even before the State of Israel was founded. Did you know, for instance, that Israel completely destroyed 418 Palestinian villages in 1948 alone? The massacre in the village of Deir Yassin by Jewish terror groups was meant to spread such fear and trauma among Palestinian inhabitants that they would pick up and leave. Palestinians in Israel were put under strict military laws for several years.

However, the year 1967 was a decisive moment in our little corner of the world. After the Six-Day War, the State of Israel occupied the West Bank, the Gaza Strip, and the Golan Heights, an occupation that goes on to this day. Over time it's taken on a deeply religious connotation. Even the name chosen for the war was meant to echo the six days of creation in Genesis. And the battle was branded by many as little "David" (the State of Israel) defeating the monster "Goliath" (the Arab World). Moreover, the conquest of East Jerusalem became the theme of the song "Jerusalem, City of Gold," 1967's top hit that popularized the image of a two thousand-year-old longing for the city. It's a song that also enshrines the myth of Israel coming back to a barren land, to dry fountains, and to the "Temple Mount."

The outcome of the 1967 war gave a boost to Jewish religious nationalism and to "messianic" extremist Jewish groups within Israel, who started settling in the West Bank, claiming it as ancient "Judea and Samaria," a designation that signaled a religious and political claim more than a geographic description. Inspired to be part of the "Judeaization" of the land, settlers started building homes on every hill with the remotest ties to biblical tradition.

The occupation of the West Bank, Gaza, and East Jerusalem gave a boost to the Israeli archeologists, who shifted their focus to the West Bank in general and to Jerusalem and the "Temple Mount" in particular. In this post-1967 discourse native Palestinian populations were seen as the Canaanites whose land had to be occupied by Israel. The Canaanites could thus be tolerated only as servants and cheap laborers under an almost-divine Jewish race. Some radical Jewish groups were openly calling for the ethnic cleansing of the Palestinian people based on biblical passages that propagated the extermination of the Canaanites and the other native groups of ancient Palestine. Jewish religious terror groups today have no problem uprooting Palestinian olive groves, attacking farmers, and vandalizing churches.

Occupation doesn't corrupt only the occupiers; it also corrupts the occupied people. State terror produces guerrilla fighters who become violent themselves, believing that they have to respond and fight back, and thinking that they can teach the occupiers a lesson. So they would engage in military operations against the occupiers and their troops. These guerrilla groups resort to the sword fully aware that they might be killed by the sword. Yet, for them this is an honor to defend their homeland and people and they see it as part of their duty and obligation. Oddly enough, the Maccabean rebels, the zealots in Jesus' day, and the Palestinian fighters are all examples of such guerrilla fighters who rise against the occupying powers.

What's more, when oppressed people realize that they are losing land, power, and people, they cling to their religion with greater fervency. Religion becomes the one thing the occupier can't take away from them. Religion becomes the most important element of their identity. They start seeing the empire as God's punishment for forgetting the divine law. For them, the empire becomes the manifestation of heathenism, which can be defeated only if God's law becomes the standard by which the people live. As a result, religious movements become obsessed with spreading the law, creating additional laws, and competing to fulfill every iota of its tenets, all as part of the strategy to overthrow the empire.

This particular response to oppression is highly attractive to an occupied people because it can produce concrete results. It is often difficult to show results by fighting the empire, but a marked increase in the number of people adhering to the law is always impressive, especially when they adhere in ways that are visible to the naked eye. The number of veiled women, the number of men with beards, and the number of people going to prayers are all quantifiable. Resorting to religion is an appealing and human response for people who feel crushed by the empire, whose dignity has been tested, and whose rights have been violated. For those who, deep down, feel that God might have forgotten about them, religious laws provide a plausible answer to the question, "Where are you, God?"

The logic goes like this: *God does not respond because we are not good enough. He has forgotten us because we have forgotten him. He has left us because we have left him. But he will return with full might if we return to his law, the sharia.* It is easy for oppressed people to become obsessed with religious laws, to hear the siren call of groups who try to take over public life by dictating etiquette—how to dress, how often to pray, and how to behave in public as well as in private. Slowly and without much noise they penetrate one social arena after the other. They start labeling what is kosher and what is not; what is halal and what is haram; what is religiously allowed and what is prohibited. Slowly they become God's spokespersons who know what is right in the eyes of God like no one else.

With time they assume the power to punish people who do not follow the law; they appoint themselves judges over people's thoughts, behavior, and actions. Such development has been seen emerging in Palestine over and over again. The Pharisees of the New Testament are a good example of such a movement. The emergence of Hamas during the first Palestinian uprising is another example of oppressed people resorting to the sharia—religious law—as the way out of oppression. And yet, these religious laws become themselves oppressive toward their own people. Jesus understood this like no other when he stated: "They tie up heavy burdens, hard to bear, and lay them on the shoulders of others" (Matt 23:4).

Once these religious movements gain enough clout, they do not hesitate to pronounce the death penalty for individuals who oppose their thinking and to eliminate anyone who dares to question their religious standing. They do all of this in the name of God and his law. They see themselves as God's servants and tools on earth. They want to make sure that they will get rid of the wicked, silence the infidel, and bring all under God's law. For them, this is a noble cause in the service of God. Notice the self-perpetuating cycle: state terror produces obsession with religious laws; the obsession with religious laws leads ultimately to religious terror; and religious terror provides a pretext for intensified state terror.

Jesus was not only a victim of state terror but also of religious terror. Jesus was not sentenced to death under Roman law alone, but probably also in the name of divine law. It was a unique combination of state terror coupled with religious terror that brought Jesus to the cross. This aspect of Jesus's death is often overlooked. Jesus was sentenced to death because he was seen as a blasphemer. He was accused of breaking the religious laws, of daring to question some of the religious practices of his time, and of challenging the religious authorities. Jesus was killed in the name of God. Those who killed him believed they were doing God a favor. Jesus was a victim of religious terrorism. The Gospel of John refers to this exact phenomenon: "An hour is coming when those who kill you will think that by doing so they are offering worship to God" (John 16:2).

Saul of Tarsus was the role model par excellence for religious terrorism. A self-proclaimed Pharisee, former Jewish leader, zealot, persecutor, and hard liner, he committed himself to making sure that God's law would prevail. He was ready to attack, terrorize, and even sanction the killing of whoever dared to question the importance of this law. He did that to Stephen and to many others as well (see Acts 8:1). For Saul, there was no compromise; he believed God's law was the only way to preserve his people's identity, demography, and security. This was the way he was brought up. This was the way he was taught. This is the way many young people are raised today in many parts of the world.

Our world today is deeply wounded by religious terrorism spawned in response to state terror. The ideological, political, and military intervention of the Soviets in Afghanistan in the late 1970s and 1980s sowed the seeds of a religiously inspired movement supported by the United States and Saudi Arabia that led in 1992 to the Islamic State of Afghanistan. With a weak government in place, even more zealous religious groups started gaining power. In 1994, the Taliban seized control of Kabul; by 1996, they declared the Islamic Emirate of Afghanistan and imposed a stricter form of religious laws similar to the one found in Saudi Arabia. The Islamic Emirate became the base for the al-Qaeda of Osama Bin Laden. The people of

Afghanistan, especially the women, became victims of religious terrorism.

A similar turn of events came in the aftermath of the 2003 American-British invasion of Iraq. The destabilization and occupation of the country created a vacuum that sparked religious movements to form. Three years after the invasion, al-Qaeda and other religious Sunni groups declared the Islamic State of Iraq. With a weakening national identity, religious Shiite, Sunni, and Kurdish identities became stronger. The road from there to ISIS was not far. ISIS terrorizes the people in the area they control in the name of God and their understanding of his religious law.

In the aftermath of the so-called Arab Spring, the Middle East has experienced a veritable mushrooming of religious terrorism. Again, state violence exercised by some Arab regimes provoked religious movements that used this opportune moment to infiltrate all aspects of society. Some of these religious groups utilize terror to get the attention of the media and to spread fear and hopelessness among masses. The execution of innocent people is captured on videos, uploaded on YouTube, and "goes viral" on the Internet.

We have to put the cross in this context of religious violence. Jesus was one of the many who experienced on his own body the violence of both state and religious terror. The cross is a permanent reminder of the millions of people who are persecuted because they don't adhere to a strict understanding of God's law. The cross is a reminder of the price many religious reformers had to pay. The cross is a reminder of all those innocent killed in the name of God.

However, the cross is more than that. If God was in Christ, then on the cross God himself was killed in the name of God. God himself becomes a victim of religious terrorism. Those who claim that God is "on their side," who are so eager to implement his laws on earth, are killing him. The cross questions all those who claim to be God's executioners on earth.

They end up executing God himself. The cross becomes a mirror that shows God's vulnerability and the cruelty of certain manifestations of human religiosity. The cross is a reminder that it is impossible to play the divine against the human, or to violate human rights in the name of divine rights. The cross is a reminder that every time human rights are violated in the name of divine rights and religious laws, God suffers.

This was Paul's great discovery. On the road to Damascus the zealot Saul had a unique encounter with no one less and nobody other than the crucified Jesus of Nazareth. This encounter transformed the radical Saul radically. This encounter made him discover that in his religious zealotry he was persecuting none other than God's own son. From that moment the zealot Saul became the passionate apostle Paul. His great discovery was that God himself in Christ has broken the walls of hostility between the human and the divine (see Eph 2:14). For Paul, this discovery had only one conclusion: If God himself in Christ and on the cross has destroyed the wall of hostility between the divine and the human, then there is no way to use religious laws to build walls between Jews and Gentiles. For Paul, the cross here was not a matter of personal salvation but of socioeconomic and political implications.

There is an urgent need today to discover this dimension of the cross. The fact that Jesus died on the cross by a combination of state and religious terror is of utmost importance as a critique of both powers. For the peoples of the Middle East, who are living either in the context of the Israeli occupation, in the context of political despotism, or are affected on a daily basis by religious extremism, this dimension of the cross is of utmost important.

In 2011, we felt at Dar al-Kalima University College a need to be more deliberate about reflecting on our context through the lens of our Christian faith. To that end we gathered a group of Christian intellectuals from six countries: Palestine, Egypt, Lebanon, Syria, Jordan, and Iraq. This process led to an ecumenical document entitled "From the Nile to the Euphrates: The Call of Faith and Citizenship,"[1] launched on December 6, 2014, in Beirut. The authors came from a variety of faith traditions, including Coptic, Maronite, Orthodox, Lutheran, Baptist, and even Muslim intellectuals.

One of the main issues highlighted in the document concerns the relationship between religion and the state, an issue that's a major challenge facing the Arab World. The authors are aware that the Middle East region "ranks last in the world for achieving a healthy relationship between religion and state" (2.1.4). The document does not speak about the separation of religion and state but instead is interested in naming an equation for a healthy relationship between the two. The authors are aware that "there is no agreement on the best principles that should govern the relationship between religion and state," and that "there is no single or unique system that may be considered ideal to form those relations" (2.1.1). The authors know that "several patterns have emerged" based on diverse "historical, cultural and social contexts of various countries" (2.1.1), and that the formulas of "both religion and state" are "constructs of historical and social" contexts and processes (2.1.2). Based on a dynamic rather than static understanding of history, the authors feel confident that a "definitive word" regarding the relationship between religion and state "has not yet been spoken," but "so long as history continues to move forward, this subject constantly needs to evolve" (2.1.3). In that sense it does not make sense to import readymade formulas from other contexts, although one could and should learn from their experiences, but instead "viable alternatives, innovative initiatives and positive contributions need to be encouraged and could help establish healthy relations" (2.1.3).

The current unhealthy relationship between religion and state is not attributed by the authors to Islam itself or Islamic theology

---

[1] "From the Nile to the Euphrates: The Call of Faith and Citizenship" (Bethlehem: Diyar, 2014).

as such, but rather—and this is unique—to the way "the ruling regimes, as well as opposition movements, manipulate religion as a tool to exert control and unilateral authority, or, conversely, to overthrow them" (2.1.4). This means that religion is being exploited for the political ends of control and access to power. Thus the prevailing unhealthy relationship is not merely a theological dilemma but also a political one; it cannot be separated from the undemocratic, patriarchal, and oppressive structures in the societies at large. Finding a healthy relationship between religion and state is thus not a mere academic exercise or luxury but is fundamental and crucial to "human progress and the development of the future of the Middle East" (2.1.5). This statement captures the authors' view:

> Disruption of a healthy balance in the relationship negatively affects the quality of life, hinders daily living, and impedes social progress. Furthermore, such disruption severely abridges the rights of minorities and women, and greatly narrows opportunities for youth. It also negates religious and intellectual pluralism, limits cultural diversity, and ultimately violates human dignity and freedom. Additionally, repressive religious systems inhibit production, squandering human potential rather than releasing and fulfilling it. (2.1.5)

This section of the document concludes by stating that "securing human dignity and well-being is at the core of religion and the ultimate *raison d'être* for statehood." Based on this statement a question arises: "Is it possible to create positive synergy between religion and state in a way that will ensure a better life for the individual in the Middle East?" (2.1.5).

The document highlights the importance of the rule of law. Both religion and the state must be under the rule of law "as a means of protection from political despotism on the one hand, and from tyrannical and repressive religious extremism that bans what it dislikes and legitimizes what suits its ambitions, on the other" (2.2.1). This issue is especially important for the Middle East, where "there is a thin and dubious line between divine laws and human legislation." The document assigns a role for religions as "value resources for constitutions, whereas a legislative authority constituted by free and fair elections must frame conventional laws that are to be upheld by an independent judiciary" (2.2.2).

What distinguishes this document, however, is its focus on the notion of citizenship. The role of the state is to safeguard the rights of all its citizens. On the other hand, religion has an important obligation to inspire its followers to undertake "full and responsible citizenship" (1.5.2). The document calls for a "conscientious and dynamic faith" that does not run away or hide from the challenges of the society but instead engages the society for the good of the state and its citizens (1.5.3). The document acknowledges the fact that there is no religious solution to the crises of the region, but that religion can be either part of the problem or part of the solution.

The cross becomes the ultimate critique of state as well as religious violence. The alternative to state and religious terror is a society based on civil laws, freedom, and equal citizenship irrespective of one's religious convictions, cultural identity, socioeconomic status, or race. This dimension of the cross is the message the world in general and the Middle East in particular is in dire need of hearing.

4

The Cross and Religious Power

The Way of Covenant Faithfulness

SUZANNE WATTS HENDERSON

All imprisonment in sacred violence is
violence done to Christ. Humankind is
never the victim of God; God is always
the victim of humankind.

—RENÉ GIRARD

"Jerusalem, Jerusalem, the city that kills the prophets and stones those who are sent to it" (Luke 13:34; see Matt 23:37). In this timeless cry Jesus anticipates his tragic fate in this matrix of religious and political power. Though the name *Jerusalem* comes from the word for "peace" *(salem)*, Jesus knows that peace sometimes comes at the cost of "sacred violence." In this sense Jesus's death in Jerusalem follows a familiar script. But it does more than that: it supplies the ultimate critique of religious violence in ways that bring freedom and hope.

Since the Holocaust scholars have downplayed religious causes behind Jesus's death, and for good reason. The first-century family debate within Judaism about Jesus's messianic status soon festered into outright Christian anti-Semitism. By the second century some Christians blamed the Jewish people for Jesus's death, and many insisted they'd replaced the Jews as God's "chosen people." Over time these views ushered in waves of religious terrorism from which the world is still reeling. From pogroms to the Inquisition to Hitler's Final Solution, history is full of "sacred violence" perpetrated by Christians against Jews, often in vindictive retribution for Jesus's death.

Thank goodness, both church and academy have faced up to this shameful legacy.[1] There can be no doubt: Jesus was executed on *political*, not religious, grounds—and by *political*, not religious, authorities. Crucifixion itself was a state-sanctioned penalty for those who threatened imperial power. To say that "the Jews" or even their leaders killed Jesus is to ignore the reality on the ground in first-century Palestine.

But it's also true that we can't fully account for Jesus's death without noting that Rome used Jerusalem's native leaders to serve Rome's political ends. Though it was surely an awkward alliance, the ruling class collaborated with their imperial overlords to preserve Jerusalem's "peace and security." Neither the Jewish people nor their leaders killed Jesus. But neither did he go to the cross without tacit support from some of Jerusalem's most influential players. How and why did this faithful Jew from Nazareth find himself at cross purposes with the guardians of his own tradition? And in what sense did his death save us from religious power and the "sacred violence" it all too often sanctions?

COVENANT FAITHFULNESS IN CONTEXT

Jesus lived and died as a first-century Palestinian Jew. But what did that religious identity mean in his own setting? What beliefs and practices marked the Second Temple Judaism to

---

[1] See the helpful collection of essays in Paula Fredriksen and Adele Reinhartz, eds., *Jesus, Judaism, and Christian Anti-Judaism: Reading the New Testament after the Holocaust* (Louisville, KY: Westminster John Knox, 2002).

which he belonged?[2] Several prominent features of his religious landscape help us see more clearly how and why Jesus might have posed a problem for some in his own religious community. Judaism stood out from other ancient religions for its exclusive loyalty to *one* God. One version of the Decalogue (Ten Commandments) opens with these words: "Hear, O Israel, the Lord is our God, the *Lord is one*" (Deut 6:4). It was this monotheism that united Jewish people wherever they lived, from modern-day Europe, to parts of Africa, and even to the Far East.

Besides monotheism, the view of Israel as God's *chosen people* provided another pillar for Second Temple Judaism. The biblical story anchors that identity in this command to Abram:

Go from your country and your kindred and your father's house to the land that I will show you. I will make of you a great nation, and I will bless you, and make your name great, so that you will be a blessing. (Gen 12:1–2)

Though Jacob (whose name God changes to Israel) doesn't appear in Genesis for two more generations, this promise to Abram confers on Jewish identity a special sense of blessing.

That foundation leads to a third feature of Second Temple Judaism: Israel's *covenant relationship* with YHWH (the proper name used for Israel's God). After saving the people from slavery in Egypt, God gives Moses the gift of Torah. In Hebrew, the word means "instruction"; in format, it's a legal code to govern the people in the promised land. Its 613 laws (including the Ten Commandments) cast religion and politics as two sides of the same coin, since they combine *exclusive allegiance to the one Lord* with provisions for a *just society*

---

[2] As the term suggests, the Jerusalem Temple standing in Jesus's day had replaced the original house of God that scripture says was built by King Solomon almost a millennium earlier. After the Babylonians destroyed the first Temple in 587 BCE, those who returned from exile in Babylon led the campaign to rebuild the structure, albeit to more modest dimensions.

that assigns value to even the weakest members. In Jesus's world Torah wasn't a way for people to *earn* God's favor; it was more like a constitution designed to reflect that favor in its sociopolitical structure.

Of course, people often violated Torah's commandments—both accidentally and with intention. So its justice system stipulated an array of sacrifices to restore the intended relationship between God and God's people. That's where the *Jerusalem Temple* comes into play. As the geographic and symbolic hub of Judaism, the Temple housed God's presence in the Holy of Holies. It also provided the only space sanctioned for priestly sacrifice. That's why, in Jesus's day, pilgrims sometimes traveled great distances—at great expense—to Jerusalem. The Temple became a locus for religious power, concentrated among the most privileged members of Jewish society.

Put simply, first-century Jews saw themselves as *a people chosen by the one God for a special covenant relationship, which they maintained by observing Torah, both in daily life and at the Jerusalem Temple.* But Second Temple Judaism was far from monolithic. Already we've mentioned Jews who resisted the Roman occupation through both sectarian withdrawal and military engagement. Other groups negotiated a way within the occupation that was less confrontational, even collaborative. In each case, though, first-century Jews did their best to live faithfully in a challenging time.

JESUS AND COVENANT FAITH: A PROPHETIC WITNESS

Jesus was not alone when he took up the cause of covenant faithfulness in a context where *both* exclusive allegiance to God *and* the marks of a just society were under siege. But he also didn't fit well with any of the main groups in the first-century landscape. How then can we understand this faithful Jew—remember, he never intended to start a new religion—in his own context?

Though the Gospels assign him many roles, from sage to rabbi to messiah, historians agree that Jesus saw himself as a prophet. Several stories portray him in this light. In one saying he implicitly identifies with "prophets [who] are not without honor, except in their hometown" (Mark 6:4; cf. Matt 13:53–58; Luke 4:16–30). Elsewhere, he cites the prophets Elijah and Elisha as biblical precedent for his own impulse to care for outsiders (Luke 4:25–27). And, as we've seen, he enters Jerusalem mindful of its reputation as a "city that kills the prophets" (Matt 23:37; Luke 13:34).

What did this prophetic role mean? Broadly speaking, biblical prophets deliver a "word from the Lord" to God's people in times of wavering faith. It's a message that calls them to realign their social and religious orders with core covenant concerns: *trust in the one God* and a *just social order*. Because their words often challenge the status quo, prophets can be wildly unpopular. King Ahab calls Elijah a "troubler of Israel" (1 Kings 18:17) and resolves to do him in. The priest Amaziah tells Amos to "go, flee away to the land of Judah, earn your bread there, and prophesy there" (Amos 7:12). They're insiders, since they're calling people to return to their own roots, but they're often seen as dangerous outsiders who bring an unwelcome message to those in charge.

Let's consider a few examples. Hosea calls Israel a "whore" who has opted for opulence over devotion to God, turning to "lovers" who "give me my bread and my water, my wool and my flax, my oil and my drink" (Hos 2:5). In place of God, Hosea says, the people are bowing at the foot of commerce—not exactly a message that would win friends among the comfortable!

For his part, Isaiah chastises Judean leaders who seek security through political alliance and weapons of war rather than through "quietness and trust" in God (Isa 30:15). In other words, they worship not YHWH but "horses" and "chariots" (Isa 31:1), that is, emblems of military might. Imagine, then, Isaiah's reception in the halls of power.

And then there's Amos, who insists that religious acts—even those prescribed in Torah—remain empty as long as the social order is rigged to raise up the rich on the backs of the poor. To those who "push the afflicted out of the way" (Amos 2:7) on the way up society's ladder, Amos brings God's scathing indictment:

> I hate, I despise your festivals,
>   and I take no delight in your solemn
>   assemblies. . . .
> But let justice roll down like waters
>   and righteousness like an ever-flowing
>   stream. (Amos 5:21, 24)

Likewise, Jeremiah sounds this warning:

> Do not trust in these deceptive words: "This is the temple of the Lord, the temple of the Lord, the temple of the Lord." For *if* you truly amend your ways and your do-ings, if you truly act justly one with another, *if* you do not oppress the alien, the orphan, and the widow, or shed innocent blood in this place, and *if* you do not go after other gods to your own hurt, *then* I will dwell with you in this place. (Jer 7:4–7, emphasis added; see also 7:15)

Jeremiah makes a provocative claim: God shows up, *even in God's house*, only when its leaders practice covenant justice.

When the prophets predict doom—and they often do—it's a direct result of covenant unfaithfulness. In this worldview the real threat to Israel's geopolitical security is an internal one: both the Assyrian victory over the Northern Kingdom in 721 BCE and the Babylonian destruction of Jerusalem in 586 BCE occur, in the prophetic script, mostly because God's people have lost their way.

But prophets also see beyond dire prediction to a more hopeful time when God will restore justice and righteousness among the people. Indeed, the darker the hour, the more the prophets amplify that hope. Parts of Isaiah written during and after the Exile promise a return to the homeland, where God's people will become a "light to the nations" (Isa 42:6; 49:6). Jeremiah says that God will write a "new covenant" on the people's hearts, and in permanent ink (Jer 31:31–34). Echoing the foundational promise that Abram was "blessed to be a blessing" (Gen 12:1–3), the prophets insist that when Israel *does* embody covenant faith, it will radiate God's glory for all the world to see (see Isa 58:9–12).

Like the prophets who have come before him, Jesus sounds a clarion call to covenant faithfulness that combines exclusive trust in God with a vision for a just world order. Like them, he warns against misplaced priorities, and so he becomes irksome to some and downright dangerous to others. Yet he also strikes a hopeful note: God is "on the loose,"[3] even in the darkest of days of foreign domination, to renew Israel and through it, the whole world.

Jesus in and around Galilee

In the Gospels the shadow of Jesus's death in Jerusalem looms over even his earliest days in the public eye (see Mark 3:6; Luke 4:29). But we know that the evangelists exaggerate—and sometimes fabricate—stories about his Jewish opponents.[4] So

---

[3] The phrase comes from Donald H. Juel, *A Master of Surprise: Mark Interpreted* (Minneapolis: Augsburg, 1994).

[4] Why the gap between Jesus's reality and the gospel story? The answer has to do with timing. Written more than three decades after Jesus's death, the Gospels postdate the Jewish War and the destruction of the Jerusalem Temple in 70 CE. With the sacrificial system in ruins the Pharisees emerged as leaders in Palestinian Judaism because they stressed everyday religious devotion over institutional religion. At the same time, tension arose between Jews who called Jesus their Messiah and mainstream leaders inclined to abandon messianic hopes altogether. It is the tension of this late-first-century conflict more than dynamics around Jesus's mission that explains the Gospels' starkly adversarial tone.

we must take great care in mining gospel sources for evidence of Jesus's threat to religious authorities in the Galilean stage of his mission. That means teasing out a few plausible tendencies against the backdrop of Jesus's own religious context.

That context, of course, features a group—notorious in the Gospels—called the "scribes and Pharisees."[5] What do we know about them? Outside the Gospels, ancient sources say that the Pharisees originated in a powerful family that ruled the land after the Maccabean Revolt (second century BCE). By Jesus's day their influence was more religious than political. Josephus calls them the "party of the people," since they fostered devotion to religious law that minimized the power of Jerusalem's priestly elite. In their own writings these teachers of the Law engage in lively, rancorous debate about how to follow Torah in daily life. Like many before and since, the rabbis took refuge from oppressive political domination by clinging to the structure found in religious law.

Their own sources offer a trustworthy glimpse into the Pharisees' dominant concerns. Chief among them was the use of Torah to strengthen Jewish identity by religious practices that distinguished them from the wider imperial culture. Take the Sabbath, for instance—a defining mark of Jewish practice. Featured among the Ten Commandments (Exod 20:8–11; Deut 5:12–15), the day of rest offers an antidote to human striving that honors God as the author and giver of life. It also set the Jewish people apart from their non-Jewish neighbors.

But while observing the Sabbath was nonnegotiable for first-century Jews, the rabbis routinely disagreed about what it did and didn't require. Jesus had his own views, which may well have drawn him into lively debate with onlookers. In one story Jesus's hungry disciples harvest their lunch on the Sabbath (Mark 2:23–28; Matt 12:1–8; Luke 6:1–5), a violation that

---

[5] The Pharisees are often called rabbis or teachers of the Law, and sometimes include scribes in their number. We use the terms interchangeably.

causes some Pharisees to confront Jesus. Though the story itself has dubious historical roots, Jesus's response may be authentic: "The Sabbath was made for humankind, not humankind for the Sabbath" (Mark 2:27). Like Amos before him, Jesus sees authentic religious devotion as a tool intended to foster, not impede, human wholeness.

Another dispute arises when Jesus heals a man on the Sabbath. To his detractors Jesus poses this question: "Is it lawful to do good or to do harm on the Sabbath, to save life or to kill it?" (Mark 3:4). Many Pharisees in his day, we should note, would have agreed with Jesus's position here. But it's also possible that some in his community grew so concerned with enforcing religious law that they lost sight of its unintended side effects. Perhaps, oddly, it was Jesus's resolute covenant faith that made him a flexible interpreter of Torah's religious practice.

Besides such boundary markers as the Sabbath, the Pharisees saw Torah's purity code as a way to safeguard the religious and cultural identity of the Jewish people. Like the Pharisees, Jesus thought matters of purity (or "holiness") extended beyond the Temple cult and into daily life. But Jesus's prophetic leanings cast the question in a sharply ethical light. When Jesus's disciples eat with unwashed hands, some accuse them of violating religious laws. But Jesus draws a provocative line between "the commandment of God" and "your tradition" (Mark 7:9), a line that distinguishes the authority of Torah itself from religious practice that interprets it. To drive his point home, Jesus accuses the rabbis of requiring payment of an offering called "Corban" (Mark 7:11) even when it leaves parents destitute and thus violates one of the Ten Commandments. In essence, Jesus interprets purity as an internal matter, not an external one (Mark 7:16); in doing so, he challenges those in his own tradition who prioritize visible boundaries that distinguish clean from unclean and righteous from unrighteous.

Indeed, Jesus's prophetic witness to covenant faith sometimes means he reframes Torah more radically. When a man asks him, "What must I do to inherit eternal life?" (Luke 10:25–37; Mark 10:17–22; Matt 19:16–22), Jesus first tells him the obvious (Jewish) answer: observe the Law. In other words, love both God and neighbor. In Luke's version Jesus goes on to tell a story about a loathed outsider who acts as "neighbor" to a man in need (Luke 10:30–36). Not only does the Samaritan embody covenant faith by caring for the injured man at great personal expense, but he also risks religious impurity to do so, since he comes into contact with human blood. In this story Jesus draws boundary lines not around ethnic identity or religious ritual but around merciful conduct. Matthew's story of the judgment of the "nations" (or "Gentiles") makes a similar point: "righteousness" comes from neither birthright nor religious observance but from meeting dire human need (Matt 25:31–46).

Jesus appears in the Gospels as a prophet who charts a course for covenant faithfulness that puts him at odds with those so devoted to religious law that they miss the human equation that law was meant to sustain. Though he came not to "abolish, but to fulfill" Torah (Matt 5:16), Jesus probably did rail against religion when it short-circuited Torah's vision of faithful community and the just world order it mandates. He may well have transgressed borders that lay, for many, at the heart of Jewish identity. Though the evangelists caricature the battle lines between Jesus and his Jewish detractors, this man who ate with "tax collectors and sinners" must have proven irksome—and possibly dangerous—to the more rigid legal experts in his path.

Jesus in Jerusalem

Jesus's visit to Jerusalem seems to have radicalized him as an outspoken critic of the establishment in ways that led to his death. We've noted that his ride into Jerusalem on a donkey and his tirade against the Temple economy probably raised concerns among the city's peacekeeping force. But what role, if any, did religious figures play in the events leading to Jesus's crucifix-ion? Can we detect any evidence that religious power may have helped to make Rome's violent ways "sacred" indeed?

Again, such questions lead us into an interpretive minefield. For reasons explained earlier, we must cast a skeptical eye on gospel sources that blame Jesus's death on Jewish leaders. Yet Jesus's prophetic message does carry with it an implicit threat to the religious establishment. Far from the sweet sage many Christians assume Jesus to be, he appears in the Gospels—espe-cially so in Jerusalem—as a hothead who defies those in charge, issuing one incendiary verbal attack after another. If religious leaders *were* at all complicit in his death, Jesus's prophetic persona makes their behavior more than plausible.

In Jerusalem religious power was concentrated in the Temple precinct and among the Sadducees, the priests, and the ruling council, with plenty of overlap among these groups. Described by Josephus as "boorish," the Sadducees were known for their elite status and for the corruption that status sometimes entailed. Their power in Judean society derived from their mediating role between religious institution and political reality. As guardians of the Temple and its sacrificial system, they wielded great authority among faithful Jews who wanted to be in right stand-ing with God. But that authority also derived in large measure from collaboration with imperial authorities; they exercised religious power only to the extent the Romans sanctioned it. By the same token, the empire depended to some extent on Jerusalem's religious leaders, who helped keep the subjugated people in check. The Temple and its officials hung in this rather delicate balance of power.

That's why it's fitting that Jesus reserves his harshest criti-cism for the Temple and all it represents. Like Jeremiah before him, Jesus's words and actions target this religious institution that implicitly sanctioned the political status quo. Besides his revolutionary disruption of the Temple economy, other stories from Jesus's last week return to this theme.

In one saying Jesus predicts the Temple's inevitable demise: "Do you see these great buildings? Not one stone will be left here upon another; all will be thrown down" (Mark 13:2; cf. Matt 24:2; Luke 21:6). Scholars think this statement is a "prediction" written with the benefit of hindsight, that is, after 70 CE, when the Romans had left the Temple in rubble visitors can see to this day. It's also possible, though, that Jesus's prophetic gaze may have seen through the "great buildings" to their corrupt and vulnerable core. Like biblical prophets before him, Jesus probably diagnosed an internal threat: as a religious institution that preyed on the vulnerable, the Temple put the holy city and its people at risk.

Besides calling out the corrupt sacrificial *system*, Jesus assails Jerusalem's religious *leaders* as well. Like the community at Qumran, Jesus thinks they've sold out to the occupying forces who authorize their power. In one curious saying Jesus curses a fig tree and then uses it as an object lesson about the ruling elite's failure to "bear fruit" (Mark 11:12–14, 20–21; cf. Jer 8:13). Elsewhere, he portrays them as "wicked tenants" (Mark 12:1–12) who perpetrate violence against the vineyard owner's messengers, including his son. Here, Jesus turns Isaiah's image of God's vineyard (Isa 5:1–7) on end, implying that Israel's leaders have forfeited the people's chosen status. Since they've ignored the terms of the relationship, he warns, "the owner of the vineyard will come and destroy the tenants and give the vineyard to others" (Mark 12:9).

Without question, these stories show signs of heavy editing by the evangelists in light of their later perspectives. Still, the weight of the evidence indicates that Jesus did condemn those *in his own tradition* who, he thought, failed to abide by the covenant.

Other gospel sayings make just this point. For instance, Jesus berates religious leaders who "like to walk around in long robes . . . and to have the best seats in the synagogues. . . . They devour widows' houses and for the sake of appearance they say long prayers" (Mark 12:38–40; Luke 20:46–47). In biblical prophecy, showing off religious power often goes hand in hand with taking unfair advantage of the poor; Jesus only echoes this perennial critique. Despite their embellished qualities these sayings help cast light on a prophetic drumbeat that would have won Jesus few friends among those in positions of religious power.

In the gospel story Jesus doesn't just speak *about* religious leaders; he confronts them directly, and with an attitude. Even before his arrest the "chief priests, the scribes, and the elders" ask him to name the source of his authority. In response, Jesus redirects their question toward his forerunner: "Did the baptism of John come from heaven, or was it of human origin?" (Mark 11:30). He sidesteps the query by connecting his own career to a more popular prophet, a move that basically silences them: "we do not know" (Mark 11:33), they reply.

In the Gospels it's not the Romans but the Jewish leaders who arrest Jesus. Judas arrives in the Garden of Gethsemane with "a crowd with swords and clubs, from the chief priests, the scribes, and the elders" (Mark 14:43; cf. Matt 26:47; Luke 22:47; John 18:3) and quickly identifies their target; "they" then apprehend him. Some think this story of an ad hoc militia is contrived, since they find it unlikely that religious leaders would have detained one of their own.

But it's possible that the religious authorities used Jesus's case to demonstrate their support for the "peace and security" Rome was trying to maintain. In this Passover setting the last thing Jewish leaders would have wanted to do was to defend a Galilean known for his stirring speeches about God's coming kingdom. Both their privileged status and the stability of the social order depended in part on defusing movements that might elicit harsh Roman reprisals. Though the Gospels overstate Jewish leaders' role in eliminating Jesus, they do provide an important window—albeit a blurry one—into the delicate dance between religion and politics in Jerusalem.

In any case, Jesus responds to this heavily armed crowd with a different kind of weapon. The group members assume they'll need to use force to apprehend him, but Jesus asks, "Have you come out with swords and clubs to arrest me as though I were a bandit?" (Mark 14:48; Luke 22:51). As one Gospel puts it, these so-called peacekeepers remain clueless about "the things that make for peace" (Luke 19:42). Like the biblical prophets Jesus casts his lot not with weaponized peace but with the "quietness and trust" (Isa 30:15) of covenant faith. It's a peace in which swords and spears become plowshares and pruning hooks (Isa 2:4); it's a peace that gives the lie to the term "sacred violence."

In the gospel story Jesus flouts religious power even more brazenly after his arrest. Gospel accounts differ about the order and number of interrogations by religious officials, but they all include the climactic moment when the high priest pronounces the charge of blasphemy that secures Jesus's death sentence on religious grounds. What's the basis of that charge? It's Jesus's response to the pointed question, "Are you the Messiah, the Son of the Blessed One?" (Mark 14:61; Matt 26:63; Luke 22:67; cf. John 18:19). The question is a curious one, since identifying as a messiah isn't in itself an act of blasphemy. But it's also a loaded question: to say a messiah has come means the earth's landscape of power is about to shift, and shift radically.

If the question is historically authentic, Jesus's real answer is lost to us. Ancient manuscripts of Mark disagree about how directly he replied; in the other Gospels he equivocates in different ways (see Matt 26:64; Luke 22:67, 70). What they *do* agree on is his prediction about the coming Son of Man "seated at the right hand of the Power" (Mark 14:62; cf. Matt 26:64; Luke 22:69; see Ps 110:1; Dan 7:13). If not outright blasphemy, it's a "messianic" prediction through and through that carries revolutionary undertones. It certainly *could* have been enough to convince the high priest of Jesus's insurgent leanings. In this way religious power may well have joined forces with state power to sanction a Roman crucifixion as an act of "sacred violence."

A final episode from the Passion story brings this dynamic into sharper relief. As Jesus hangs on the cross, passersby openly taunt him: "Save yourself, and come down from the cross" (Mark 15:30). Religious leaders also scoff that "he saved others; he cannot save himself. Let the Messiah, the King of Israel, come down from the cross now, so that we may see and believe" (Mark 15:31–32). For the evangelists the words are ironic on many levels—in part because they harken back to Jesus's warning against saving oneself (see Mark 8:35–36).

But they also telegraph an interplay between religion and violence that's all too familiar. Those who cheer Jesus's executioners and mock the dying criminal do so because their *religious* worldview is shaped by the dominant *social and political* discourse, rather than the other way around. In Jesus's case the Roman Empire controls the discourse that links crucifixion to the weakest, most despised members of society. As long as imperial power prevails, religious power remains its captive. For many onlookers, Jesus's crucifixion by Roman authorities only confirms that he is another bogus messiah in their midst.

THE WAY OF THE CROSS: FROM RELIGION TO FAITH

In the gospel story Jesus's execution as a political criminal exposes religion's tendency toward "sacred violence" that makes God a victim of humankind. True, crucifixion was a capital sentence under imperial, not religious, jurisdiction. But religious leaders whose only power came from imperial overlords probably collaborated with Rome to silence Jesus when his radical call to covenant faithfulness threatened both their own privilege and the stable social order on which it depended. As a result, Jesus's call went silent, at least in the short run.

But for a small group of followers the cross soon denoted not Jesus's messianic failure but the messianic momentum he set in motion. In his death they detected a bold covenant faithfulness that exposed the "clear and present danger" of religious power coopted by empire. In the cross they found an enduring example that saves us from the "sacred violence" that persists to this day.

How does Jesus's resolute faith renew and reclaim religious power? For one thing, his radical *trust in God's power* is more than a matter of belief. It means he takes his marching orders from God's reign and so becomes its agent wherever destructive forces raise an ugly head. Religion often marks the sacred from the profane, the pure from the impure, the insider from the defilement of the outsider. But Jesus consistently elides religious distinction as he channels God's saving power where it's most needed. He touches lepers; he eats with tax collectors and sinners; he keeps company with those whose inner demons make them unfit for human society. Sometimes he even violates religious protocol. For Jesus, covenant faith runs deeper than religious performance or doctrinal belief; covenant faith means aligning with God's power to make the world new.

Outside the Gospels, Jesus's covenant faith lies at the heart of Paul's theology of the cross and its saving power. For Paul, the cross epitomizes Christ's faithfulness as the event that turns the world toward God's righteous ways. Paul himself is a former Pharisee whose devotion to Torah is beyond reproach (see Phil 3:5). "Yet," he says, "we know that a person is justified [made righteous] not by the works of the law but through [the faith of Jesus Christ]" (Gal 2:16).[6] For Paul, the contrast is stark.

Scholars think the "works of the law" are identity markers (circumcision, dietary laws, and religious festivals) that set the

---

[6] The phrase "faith of Jesus Christ" is a more natural reading of the genitive Greek phrase *pistis iesou christou*. Christian tradition has often translated the phrase as "faith in Jesus Christ," but contemporary interpreters increasingly acknowledge that this reading alters Paul's intent to focus on Christ's saving faith.

Jewish people apart from their Gentile neighbors. But Paul detects in Christ's faith a stunning new identity marker for God's people. It's a faith that breaks down religious and social barriers rather than building them up (Rom 3:22; Gal 2:18; 3:28). It's a faith that reclaims the divine "DNA" in God's "children" (Rom 8:14–17; Gal 3:26). It's a faith that even takes on a curse rooted in religious law and nullifies it (Gal 3:13; cf. Deut 21:23). Finally, it's Christ's covenant faith that sets the terms for our faith as well.

In this way Paul thinks Jesus's death redeemed the world from the unholy alliance between religion and conventional power by promoting covenant faith. Indeed, his letter to the Romans expresses the gospel in these terms:

> It is the power of God for salvation to everyone who has faith, to the Jew first and also to the Greek. For in it the righteousness of God is revealed through faith for faith; as it is written, "The one who is righteous will live by faith." (Rom 1:16–17)

For Paul, the saving power of Jesus's faith cuts through religious distinction to activate a cross-shaped faith—a faith that trusts God's power more than the power of the empire.

In the generations after Jesus's death those who called him Lord and Christ took seriously his call to covenant faithfulness. Like their Jewish counterparts, they affirmed loyalty to the one God of Israel. They also gained a reputation for caring for the poor and vulnerable, not just among their communities but in the wider society as well. Both commitments sometimes endangered their very lives. But in Jesus's example of covenant faith and his emphatic unwillingness to deploy violence to defend that faith, they found salvation and hope.

All of that began to change when Christianity became the state-sanctioned religion of the Roman Empire. Legend has it that Constantine's fourth-century conversion to Christianity came from a battlefield vision in which Christ charged him to "conquer in my name." The alliance of church and state that followed has left a deep stain on the Christian legacy. Church leaders have often overlooked Jesus's radical witness to covenant faith, opting instead for conventional power that has its roots in a culture of division and death. Once Christian power coalesced around issues of ritual, dogma, and even ethnicity, it has worked hand in glove with political power to identify, subjugate, and sometimes eliminate the "other." In this shift "sacred violence" has all too often replaced covenant faith and, I dare say, robbed the cross of part of its saving power.

CONCLUDING THOUGHTS

As we stand on the threshold of a post-Christian era, we're well positioned to consider anew some hopeful questions: What if we took seriously Jesus's prophetic call to covenant faithfulness? What if we embraced the early Christian refusal to participate in systems of sacred violence? What if the church modeled for our world both unflinching trust in God's saving power and deep concern for those who most need that power? What if we acted as if the "things that make for peace" (Luke 19:42) have nothing to do with arsenals or battle plans but everything to do with justice and righteousness and faith?

These questions may seem farfetched, but history offers glimpses of those who have taken an alternative, cross-shaped approach to resisting oppressive systems supported in part by religious power. What's stunning is that we fail to take into account just how successful they have been. Jesus's example of covenant faithfulness animated the Confessing Church in its subversive stand against Nazi Germany. It provided a vision for South Africans leading the way into a post-apartheid world. Even today, leaders around the globe step up to "sacred violence" not with swords and clubs but through words and deeds that bring life and hope and peace. Jesus saves indeed.

But we don't have to look abroad to see instances of religious violence from which we still need redemption. As a country, we've not yet owned the church's endorsement of "sacred violence" against people of color and others outside the bounds of our doctrines or our church walls. That violence has sometimes been physical: burning crosses and lynching trees come to mind, as does the plague of child abuse by religious figures. But the violence has also been emotional and psychological, as authorities cling to religious law in ways that relegate so many to outsider status. It's no wonder that some have come to equate Christianity with constraint more than with freedom.

The good news for our place and time is that Jesus died, in part, to save us from any religion that would use its power to separate people from one another and, in the process, kill the body or the spirit. On the cross he put an end to this curse by modeling the full measure of covenant faith—a trust in God that can't help but spill out in justice that rolls down "like waters, and righteousness like an ever-flowing stream" (Amos 5:24). It's part of the good news, I think, our world is longing to hear.

5

The Journey from Death to Life

The Poetry of Mahmoud Darwish

MITRI RAHEB

It is interesting to see that the cross is a theme found in the writings of so many Palestinian poets and writers, both Christians and Muslims. There must be something there that gave all those writers inspiration, courage, and hope. There must be something powerful there that whenever the Palestinian people were looking for metaphors and symbols to represent their identity, their struggle, and their context, they could not find any other metaphor that was more powerful and suitable than the cross.

The most prominent Palestinian poet in modern history was without a doubt Mahmoud Darwish. Mahmoud Darwish was born in 1941 to a Palestinian Muslim family in the village of Birweh, in Galilee. When he died in 2008, almost every Palestinian was acquainted with his poetry and had committed at least some of it to memory, since his poems were turned into popular songs that people across the Arab World sang by heart.

An older version of this chapter was published as "Biblical Narrative and Palestinian Identity in the Works of Mahmoud Darwish's Writings," in *Palestinian Identity in Relation to Time and Space,* ed. Mitri Raheb (Bethlehem: Diyar, 2014), 89–105.

And yet, no other Palestinian poet referred to the cross and the passion story like Darwish.

If his name had not been Mahmoud, I would have thought him a Christian theologian, a scholar well versed in the biblical narrative, or even an Old Testament prophet who could capture in poetic words the hopes and fears of his people and bring to them God's words in their context. In his poetry he wrote about the Samaritan woman,[1] Mary Magdalene,[2] as well as the woman who poured perfume on Jesus' feet.[3] Moreover, he took examples from the Old Testament and mentioned Joseph and his brothers,[4] Abraham,[5] Ishmael,[6] Joshua, son of Nun,[7] David and Solomon,[8] the Song of Solomon,[9] Job,[10] Cain and Abel,[11] the land flowing with milk and honey,[12] Sodom and Gomorrah,[13] Lot,[14] Noah,[15] Isaiah,[16] and Habakkuk.[17] His poetry also notes the birth of Jesus, his baptism, his transfiguration,[18] his teachings, his first miracle

---

[1] *The Complete Poems: The Mahmoud Darwish Anthology,* vol. 1–2, From "Bed of a Stranger" (1996–97): "I Waited for No One."

[2] Recorded poem: "In Praise of the High Shadow" (1983).

[3] From "Bed of a Stranger (1996–1997): "I Waited for No One."

[4] From "Fewer Roses" (1986): "Oh, My Father, I Am Yusuf."

[5] From "Why Did You Leave the Horse Alone": "The Eternity of Cactus."

[6] From "Why Did You Leave the Horse Alone": "Strangers' Walk."

[7] From "Why Did You Leave the Horse Alone": "How Many Times Will It Be Over."

[8] "Jidariyya (Mural)" (1999).

[9] From "Eleven Planets" (1992): "The Speech of the Red Indian."

[10] "Jidariyya (Mural)" (1999); "In Praise of the High Shadow."

[11] "Jidariyya (Mural)" (1999); "Why Did You Leave the Horse Alone"; "The Raven's Ink."

[12] "Almond Blossoms and Beyond."

[13] From "End of the Night" (1967): "A Woman from Sodom."

[14] "Jidariyya (Mural)" (1999).

[15] From "Lover from Palestine" (1966): "Waiting for the Returning Refugees."

[16] Recorded poem: "In Praise of the High Shadow" (1983).

[17] From "Lover from Palestine" (1966): "Anthem."

[18] "Almond Blossoms and Beyond"; "Mural."

in Cana when he turned water into wine,[19] the parable of the Vineyard,[20] and his walking on water.[21] Nothing, though, was as powerful as his writings about the crucifixion and resurrection.[22] The names of many of his poems signal their resonance with biblical themes and stories: "Hallelujah"; "My God, My God, Why Have You Forsaken Me?"; "Love Is Strong as Death"; "Vanity of Vanities."

In one of his last interviews with the newspaper *Al Hayat*, our great poet was asked: "Speaking of religion, we notice that your poetry has some biblical influence, observed particularly in Nashid al-Anshad ("Song of Songs") in the lyrical content of Sareer al-Ghareeba ("Bed of the Stranger"), as well as others. Why has the biblical text interested you as a poet, and how has it affected you?"

Darwish replied: "First, I studied in Occupied Palestine. We were required to study some of the text of the Torah in Hebrew, and so I did. With that being said, I do not contemplate the Torah from a religious or historical perspective, but consider it rather as a work of literature." Darwish sounds here almost like a modern historical-critical Christian theologian.

He was then asked the direct question: "Is the Bible one of your sources?"

Darwish answered without hesitation: "There is no doubt that it is one of my literary sources."

This was followed by another question: "Have you reread the Torah in Arabic?"

His answer was: "Yes, I read several Arabic translations of it, including some recent ones of which I especially enjoy the plain ones. Such texts have to be translated in a very particular way.

---

[19] From "Why Did You Leave the Horse Alone": "The Eternity of Cactus."

[20] From "Fewer Roses": "God, Why Have You Forsaken Me?"

[21] "Jidariyya (Mural)" (1999).

[22] From "End of the Night" (1967): "Naive Song on the Red Cross"; and from "Leaves of Olives" (1964), including "To the Reader," "Allegiance," "On Man," "On Steadfastness," "*Rubaiyyat*."

Nashid al-Anshad ("Song of Songs") has been considered by some great universal poets as one of the most highly acclaimed pastoral songs in the history of poetry, despite its Pharaonic and Assyrian influences."[23]

Whoever reads this interview is certain to be surprised that Darwish had read the Bible in several languages, several translations, and several times! One might wonder: Did our poet underestimate the value of the Bible? After all, he declared that he perceived the Bible strictly as a work of literature and not as a religious or historical text. While this may seem to be the case at first glance, and on the surface, once we realize that in the mindset of the poet nothing but literature is immortal, we grasp that while describing the Bible as a "historical" or "religious" text may have sounded sophisticated, his portrayal of it as a work of literature renders it mighty and divine.

I was interested to read all of Mahmoud Darwish's poems from the first to the last with the intention of seeing how and when Darwish quotes from the biblical narrative in general and when in his life journey he refers to the cross in particular. I am able to depict four different stages in his life, indicating his context—whether Palestinian, international, or his own personal context. There is no doubt that Darwish was one of our brilliant contextual theologians. In each of these stages specific literary texts dominate Darwish's thinking. Indeed, for every context in his life journey and that of his people Darwish finds that biblical text that gives him inspiration!

The First Stage: 1964–1967

The young Darwish, exiled from the village of Birweh in his early twenties, lived in Haifa and felt oppressed, persecuted, and imprisoned, yet he persisted. At this stage he saw in the crucified Jesus a reflection of himself—a freedom fighter who endured suffering but who rose again. In three of his first four poems

---

[23] Minfo.gov.ps/Docs/dialogs.asp.

the cross makes such a pronounced appearance that those who read Darwish's words will think they were written by a Latin American liberation theologian. Those of us who have memorized his poems in the lyrics of Marcel Khalife have perhaps not considered the considerable liberation theology emanating from them. His poem "Ecce Homo" provides just such an example.

> They fettered his mouth with chains,
> And tied his hands to the rock of the dead.
> They said: You're a murderer.
> They took his food, his clothes and his
> banners,
> And threw him into the well of the dead.
> They said: "You're a thief."[24]

> You, with the bloody eyes and palms,
> The night is soon to be gone,
> The detention room won't last,
> Nor will the chains,
> Nero died, but Rome did not,
> With her eyes, she fights.
> A withered spike will die,
> And will nourish the whole valley.[25]

In this poem Darwish identifies fully with the Crucified. He, like him, is innocent of any wrongdoing. It is the occupying power that is violating the law. But Darwish is certain that the cross is not an end in itself, that this death on the cross will bear life for many.

And in the poem "The Singer Said" he recounts:

---

[24] Translation source: Peter Clark, "Mahmoud Darwish: Poet, Author and Politician Who Helped to Forge a Palestinian Consciousness after the Six-Day War in 1967," *The Guardian* (August 11, 2008).

[25] From "Leaves of Olives" (1964): "On Man"; and from *Mahmoud Darwish Anthology*, vol. 1–2.

The singer on the cross,
his wound glowing like a star
expressed everything to the people
around him, everything except regret:
This way I have died as I stand
and standing I die like a tree.
This way my cross becomes
a platform or a maestro's baton.
This way the nails of this cross
become musical chords.
This is how rain falls,
this is how trees grow.[26]

In this poem the meaning of the cross is unmistakable: it stands for the path of redemption; the juncture of struggle; and the only way of salvation. The cross is not a sign of surrender or defeat but it is a sign of resistance. The wounds of the Crucified share a positive message, a message sweet like redemption.

Another example of this stage is found in his poem "Nashīd (Anthem)"[27]:

Hello?
I want Jesus
What! Who are you?
I am speaking from Israel
I have nails in my feet,
I carry a wreath of thorns
Which path do I choose
Oh man, which path?
Do I do penance for sweet salvation
Or do I walk on?
Do I walk on, or do I die?
I say to you: March on, men!

---

[26] Translation source: Khaled Mattawa, "When the Poet Is a Stranger" (2009).
[27] From "Lover from Palestine" (1966): "Anthem."

Again in this poem Darwish carries his cross. Feeling fatigued and doubtful, he hears the words of Jesus that give him the courage to continue his struggle and walk towards Golgotha. In this first stage the last mention of the cross is found in the poem "A Love Song on the Cross," in which the Crucified speaks to his lover: the city of Jerusalem.

> I love you
> Be my cross
> Be, as you wish, a dove tower
> If your hands were to dissolve me
> They would fill the desert with shroud.[28]

The cross is also significant here: it represents enduring love and serves as a message for goodness, tenderness, and everlasting peace for humankind. Darwish wrote this poem the same year Jerusalem was captured and while he was held under house arrest.

Religious symbolism becomes dull in his poetry after the fall of Jerusalem in 1967, as though he had lost his speech and narrative due to the Naksah and the defeat of that war resulting in the occupation of the West Bank and the Gaza Strip. At this stage Darwish joined the Communist Party, left for Moscow, went to Egypt, and finally traveled to Beirut, where he settled. In the period between the fall of Jerusalem in 1967 and the siege of Beirut in 1982, our poet avoided mentioning the biblical narrative and stayed away from religious metaphors. After all, he was now a Communist and unconcerned with parables. In those fifteen years his inspiration derived from the Crucified was replaced by his socialist beliefs and connection with the Soviet Union. Nevertheless, the parable eventually outplayed communism, and divine influence took over once again. There was no way for him to escape the cross, which was present from the first moment ink touched paper and words were set in motion.

---

[28] Ibid.

In this first stage of Darwish's work, we can distinguish the liberation theologian who uses the image of the Crucified as a prototype to symbolize the Palestinian prisoner and martyr who stands against defeat and subjugation, carries his cross, and sacrifices his own blood for a better future. There is no reference to the biblical narrative in his collections from 1967 to 1982, up until the siege of Beirut and the massacre of Sabra and Shatila in 1982, when suddenly the poet's inspiration returned.

The Second Stage: 1982–1992

In 1982 the Palestinian Liberation Organization and its members were besieged in Beirut by the Israeli forces. Some Lebanese forces were compliant with the Israeli forces and massacred Palestinians in the refugee camps of Sabra and Shatila. At last the PLO and their fighters had to leave Lebanon and go to Tunisia. What the Palestinian people faced and endured in Beirut, especially from the Lebanese forces and other Arab countries who did not come to assist the Palestinians, may be similar to the sense of abandonment that Jesus on the cross came up against from those closest to him:

> They reduced him, denounced him, they
>   deserted him,
> they left him on the cross
> and placed him in the tomb,
> they besieged him between gravestones.
> They broke you, oh how they broke you,
> to make a throne out of your anguish,
> They split you, denounced you, they
>   concealed you
> and made an army out of your distress,
> They put you in the gravestone and said: do
>   not turn over

They threw you in the well and said: do not
    turn over
You greeted your battle, my mother's son
A thousand years, a thousand years in the
    sun,
They denounced you, for all they know is
    how to rattle and run
They now rob you of your skin.
Watch out from the likes of them, my
    mother's son
You who are more than a father's son
Oh how alone you are.[29]

In another example from this poem, Mahmoud writes:

Allahu Akbar,
This verse is ours.
Read
In the name of the rebel who birthed
    sympathy
out of his pain
In the name of the rebel who withdraws
from your time
to follow his first call
the first and the first
We'll destroy the temple
In the name of the rebel who begins
Read
Our portrait is Beirut
Our *Sura* is Beirut.[30]

In this poem Darwish links the Qur'an and the Bible as if he
were a prophet who received a *Sura* entitled "Beirut." He reads

---

[29] Recorded poem: "In Praise of the High Shadow" (1983).
[30] Ibid.

his poem as the rebel who gave birth to sympathy out of his pain and who was called to destroy the Temple in order to build it in three days.

Whoever reads "In Praise of the High Shadow" will find it filled with biblical metaphors related to Job, Adam—who was cast out of paradise like the Palestinians who left Beirut, Mary Magdalene, Isaiah—who lamented Jerusalem, and many other symbols and verses.

The second stage of Darwish's life starts with the siege of Beirut and continues until a little before the Oslo Accords. This is a pivotal stage. After Beirut, Palestinians felt abandoned by the other Arab nations. They felt alone. Palestine was sold by the Arabs like Yusuf ("Joseph") had been sold by his brothers:

> Oh my father, I am Yusuf
> Oh father, my brothers neither love me nor
>   want me in their midst
> They assault me and cast stones and words
>   at me
> They want me to die so they can eulogize me
> They closed the door of your house and left
>   me outside
> They expelled me from the field
> Oh my father, they poisoned my grapes . . .
> What have I done, Oh my father?
> Why me?
> You named me Yusuf and they threw me into
>   the well
> They accused the wolf
> The wolf is more merciful than my brothers
> Oh, my father
> Did I wrong anyone when I said that
> I saw eleven stars and the sun and the moon
> Saw them kneeling before me?[31]

---

[31] From "Fewer Roses" (1986): "Oh My Father, I Am Yusuf." Translated from the Arabic by Fady Joudah.

This is an interesting poem. At this stage and in the context of the siege in Beirut, Darwish felt that the Arab states were just pitying the Palestinian people. They got used to seeing in them mere victims to eulogize. This wasn't Darwish's understanding of the cross or of the Palestinian people. The Crucified is not a dead person to eulogize.

Another factor that made this a decisive stage in Darwish's life was the fall of the Soviet Union, which came as a shock for committed Communists who saw the world come crashing down before their eyes.

Faced with the betrayal of the Arab World on the one hand and the fall of the Soviet Union on the other, Darwish felt abandoned by everyone, including God. Yet it is at this stage particularly that he begins a conversation with God, applying suggestive metaphors of prayer, such as the prayer in the Garden of Gethsemane before the Last Supper, and the prayer of Jesus on the cross, as illustrated by two examples:

> My God, my God, why have you forsaken
>   me? Why did you wed Mary?[32]
> Why did you pledge my only tender to the
>   army—Why?
> I, the widow, the daughter of this stillness,
>   the daughter of your jilted word–
> Why have you forsaken me?
> My God, my God, why did you wed Mary?
> You set down two nations from a spike
> And wed me to a conception, and I complied;
> complied with your forthcoming wisdom
> Have you dismissed me, or have you set off
>   to heal the other,
> my enemy, from the guillotine?
> Does she, she who is the same as I,
> Does she have the right to ask to wed God?

---

[32] Mary here is a metaphor for Israel.

and to ask God, my God, why have you
    forsaken me?
Why did you wed me, Lord? Why, why did
    you wed Mary?[33]

The Last Supper lingers, so do the Last
    Supper commandments,
Father, be full of grace with us,
Wait for us a little while, oh Lord!
Do not pull out the glass from us,
Take it slow, so that we may ask more than
    we have asked.[34]

At this stage Jesus is no longer seen as the rebel in search of
a redemptive death, but rather as the son looking for another
chance in life. The withering spikes that will nourish the whole
valley are not what matter at this point. On the contrary, Darwish switches from a theology concerned with martyrdom to a
theology of martyria that celebrates life. In this period before
the first Intifada we find him to be wary of speeches that might
hail the victim. From now on Darwish's interest is not to die
for Palestine, but to live for his country.

They'd love to see me dead, so they can say:
he was one of us, he belonged to us.[35]
It is also at this stage that he proclaims:
"We have on this earth what makes life
    worth living."[36]

The Third Stage: 1993–1989

In the third stage, which coincided along with the Oslo Accords, Darwish's rationale was the same as Edward Said's: he

---

[33] From "Fewer Roses" (1986): "God, Why Have You Forsaken Me?"
[34] From "Fewer Roses" (1986): "The Last Supper Lingers."
[35] From "Fewer Roses" (1986): "They'd Love to See Me Dead."
[36] From "Fewer Roses" (1986): "We Have on This Earth What Makes
Life Worth Living."

was opposed to the Accords. And yet he agrees to resettle and to return from his exile to Palestine, because "on Palestinian soil" there is something worthwhile living for. In this period there is a great deal of symbolism alluding to Genesis as Darwish draws metaphors from Oslo to the equality between Cain and Abel; the oppressor and the victim.[37] He also makes the comparison of self-sacrifice as drawn from the example of Abraham and his son (Ishmael).[38]

The Fourth Stage: 1999–2008

The fourth and final stage of Darwish's life began around 1999. The context changes just as Darwish's personal context also changed drastically. After undergoing open-heart surgery in Paris, Darwish found himself in a hospital between life and death, between existence and nothingness, and in a battle between body and spirit. He was convinced that his death was still not imminent.[39] It was neither harvest time nor the day of judgment.

As Darwish found himself battling with death, he sought to understand the true meaning of life and speculated about whether he should follow Solomon's wise path or Christ's rising from the dead. Darwish chose Solomon, the wise king, whose glory the poet identified with but whose path he nevertheless recognized as vain and ephemeral.

Darwish identifies with Solomon so much in this period that he almost seems to replicate Solomon's path, yet he finds it difficult to identify with Jesus when death advances on him.[40]

> And wait
> A child will carry your soul in your place
> immortality is procreation nothing less

---

[37] From "Why Did You Leave the Horse Alone": "The Raven's Ink."
[38] From "Why Did You Leave the Horse Alone": "Abel's Space"/"Ishmael's *Oud.*"
[39] "Jidariyya (Mural)" (1999).
[40] Ibid.

everything is vain or ephemeral
ephemeral or vain
Who am I?
The Song of Songs?
or the wisdom of Ecclesiastes?
You and I are me
I'm poet
and king
and a wise man at the edge of the well
No cloud in my open hand
in my temple no eleven planets
my body narrow
my eternity narrow
and my tomorrow sitting like a crown of dust
        on my throne
Vain vanity of vanities . . . vain
Everything on earth is ephemeral
The winds are north
the winds are south
The sun rises by itself and sets by itself
nothing is new
The past was yesterday
futile in futility
The temple is high
and the wheat is high
If the sky comes down it rains
and if the land rises up it's destroyed
Anything that goes beyond its limits will
        become its
opposite one day
And life on earth is a shadow of something
        we can't see
Vanity vanity of vanities . . . vain
Everything on earth is ephemeral
1,400 chariots

12,000 horses
Carry my gilded name from one age to
    another
I lived as no other poet
a king and sage
I grew old and bored with glory
I didn't lack for anything
Is this why the more my star rose the more
    my anxiety grew?
So what's Jerusalem and what's a throne
if nothing remains forever?
There's a time for birth
and a time for death
A time for silence
and a time for speech
A time for war
and a time for peace
and a time for time
nothing remains forever
Each river will be drunk by the sea
and the sea still is not full
Nothing remains forever
everything living will die
and death is still not full
Nothing will remain after me except a gilded
    name:
'Solomon was ...'
So what do the dead do with their names?
Is it the gold
or the song of songs
or the Ecclesiastes
who will illuminate the vastness of my
    gloom?
Vanity vanity of vanities . . . vain
everything on earth is ephemeral

I saw myself walking like Christ on the lake
but I came down from the cross because of
    my fear of heights
and I don't preach the resurrection.[41]

Darwish did not in fact fear heights; he feared death. He had a hard time believing in the resurrection, yet with this lack of faith, life was deemed meaningless. In "Jidariyya (Mural)," Darwish discovers what one man is able to keep in the face of death and ends his poem by saying:

This name is mine . . .
and also my friends' wherever they may be
And my temporary body is mine
present or absent...
Two metres of this earth will be enough for
    now
a metre and 75 centimetres for me
and the rest for flowers in a riot of colour
who will slowly drink me
And what was mine is mine: my yesterday
and what will be in the distant tomorrow in
    the return
of the fugitive soul
as if nothing has been
and as if nothing has been
A light wound on the arm of the absurd
    present
History taunting its victims
and its heroes...
throwing them a glance and passing on
This sea is mine

---

[41] Ibid. Translated from the Arabic by Rema Hammami and John Berger ("Mural," 46–48).

This sea air is mine
And my name—if I mispronounce it on my
   coffin—is mine
And as for me—full of all reasons for
   leaving—
I am not mine
I am not mine
I am not mine.[42]

When death drew near, Darwish realized that he did not have ownership of himself and he confessed that, after all, he had no control over his destiny.

While his proficiency in the Old Testament and the Gospels is obvious to the reader, Darwish seems not to have been acquainted with Paul, whose name is nowhere mentioned in his poetry. Paul himself had a similar experience of realizing that we do not live for ourselves, which is added to his faithful perception that "whether we live or whether we die, we are the Lord's" (Rom 14:8).

While Darwish stops at "I am not mine" and does not go further, Paul writes: "We do not live to ourselves, and we do not die to ourselves. . . . We are the Lord's" (Rom 14:7–8). Darwish wasn't able here to experience what Paul talked about when he wrote:

"Where, O death, is your victory?
   Where, O death, is your sting?" (1 Cor
   15:55)

Darwish's poetry did not cease with "Mural" in 1999. He kept pondering the mysteries of life and death in his last eight years, as exemplified in his final collection of poetry, "Almond

---

[42] Ibid. Translated from the Arabic by Rema Hammami and John Berger ("Mural," 54).

Blossoms and Beyond," in which he no longer fantasizes about his great hopes but is beginning to grasp the meaning of life through its subtle nuances:

> It is said: Love is as strong as Death.
> I say: But lust for life, even with no
> 　　satisfying proofs,
> is stronger than Life and Death.
> So let us end our private funeral rite
> and share with our neighbors in song.
> Life is axiomatic . . . and true as dust.[43]

In his last years Darwish saw himself on a bridge swathed in dense fog. Similar to the Israelites, he would need to cross the River Jordan to end his exile and reach the Promised Land.[44] During his last days on this bridge he witnessed with faithful eyes that which he had never seen before. Thus he resolved that "every place far from God and His earth is an exile," and "in a world that has no heaven, the earth becomes an abyss":[45]

> Shout so that you hear yourself, shout so that
> 　　you know
> that you are still alive, and you know that life
> 　　is possible on this earth.
> Invent a hope for words, or an area, or a
> 　　mirage,
> to prolong hope.
> And sing, for beauty is freedom.
> I say: Life defined only as the opposite of
> 　　death is not life.[46]

---

[43] From "Almond Blossoms and Beyond": "A Wedding Over There." Translated from the Arabic by Mohammad Shaheen.

[44] From "Almond Blossoms and Beyond": "Exile (2)."

[45] From "Almond Blossoms and Beyond": "Exile (3)."

[46] From "Almond Blossoms and Beyond": "Exile (4)."

This was one of Darwish's last poems. Here Darwish sees in himself almost a messenger or a prophet who in the face of a nearing death was sent to proclaim life, hope, and freedom.

Those who read Darwish from start to finish will find a man who lived in the biblical narrative, a narrative that was not a fleeting phase in the poet's life but a source of inspiration that influenced him so markedly that he used it at every juncture. For Darwish, the biblical narrative of ancient times in general and the cross in particular was but the metaphor of the Palestinian people today. Darwish, the Palestinian Muslim, was able to identify with the cross because he sensed that the cross is the best expression of his people's identity. While at the beginning of his life and as a young fighter himself, the cross was a symbol of martyrdom and dying for Palestine, the older that Darwish gets the more he starts understanding martyria as a call to live for his cause. Faced with death himself, Darwish realizes that the calling of both poet and prophet is to proclaim life, to spread hope, and to live for others. With this conviction Darwish crossed from the cross to the resurrection.

6

The Cross and Personal Power

The Way of Sacrificial Servanthood

SUZANNE WATTS HENDERSON

*If physical death is the price I must pay
to free my white brothers and sisters from
the permanent death of the spirit, then
nothing could be more redemptive.*

—MARTIN LUTHER KING, JR.

So far, we've reflected on the cross's saving power in the face
of political and religious authorities bent on violence. But our
discussion of political and religious systems leads to another
important question: How does Jesus's death save us not just
from forces outside our direct control but also *from our very
selves*? In this chapter we explore the kind of personal power
that's reframed and redeemed on the cross.

We should say at the outset that the discussion that follows
cuts against the grain of popular Christianity in at least two
ways. For one thing, it's not *just* about heaven, at least as a des-
tination when we die. It's about how we exercise our personal
power, every day. For another thing, it's not *just* about Jesus
and what he did for us, as if we're not part of God's grand plan
of redemption. It's about the contours of his power in life and

death and the ways in which that power is, by grace, at work in and through us today.

After all, when Jesus describes the marching orders for his disciples, he uses language that forges close connections between his journey and ours. Jesus puts it this way:

> If any want to become my followers, let them deny themselves and take up their cross and follow me. For those who want to save their life will lose it, and those who lose their life for my sake, and for the sake of the gospel, will save it. (Mark 8:34–35; see Matt 10:38–39; Luke 14:27, 17:33; John 12:25)

It's not just Jesus who is called to "come and die," as Bonhoeffer put it.[1] Jesus's saving death becomes a model of personal power for his disciples in every place and time.

On one level Jesus's words may sound like sheer nonsense at best and deeply harmful at worst. As theologian James Cone asks: "Have not blacks, women, and poor people throughout the world suffered enough? Giving value to suffering seems to legitimize it."[2] All too often so-called authorities use the cross to sanction personal power that's coercive or even deadly. Abused spouses and children are told their suffering is a "cross to bear." Religious leaders interpret self-denial as a mandate for self-loathing. And soldiers "take up a cross" as a reminder that God is on their side. It's no wonder that Christians and non-Christians sometimes bristle at the saying as a call to martyrdom.

But what if, instead, it's a call to martyria—to the kind of witness Darwish expressed in the simple phrase "I am not my own"? What if, rather than browbeating people into submission, Jesus invites us to willing self-sacrifice that locates our personal

---

[1] Dietrich Bonhoeffer, *Cost of Discipleship*, trans. R. H. Fuller (1959; New York: Touchstone, 1995), 89.

[2] James Cone, *The Cross and the Lynching Tree* (Maryknoll, NY: Orbis Books, 2011), 92.

power not in self-concern but in God's wider landscape of redemption? What if "losing life" means losing our *selves* in service to the cause of God's beloved people? Could this be one of the ways Jesus's death saves us?

SACRIFICIAL SERVANTHOOD IN CONTEXT

Most Jews in Jesus's day thought his shameful destiny proved either that God had abandoned him or that he was a fraud. They didn't expect to see God's son hanging on a Roman cross. They assumed God's messiah would have enough personal power to overwhelm imperial power, not be crushed by it. Most of their own traditions told them as much.

Yet a scant few *were* convinced that Jesus's death had set God's renewal of the earth in motion. Oddly enough, they'd seen God in a tortured body heaving for every last breath. How to make sense of such a senseless fate? How might Jesus's execution have revealed God's dream for the world? How might personal power have been evident in his death, rather than extinguished by it?

To answer these questions, they followed Jesus deep into the context of his own Jewish tradition. As Jesus had, they gravitated toward texts forged in the fires of subjugation and oppression. There, they found liberating power in *servanthood* and *sacrifice* as lenses that brought redemptive suffering into focus.

Redemptive Servanthood in Second Isaiah

The writer of Isaiah 40—55 grapples with questions that emerge during the Babylonian Exile: Has God abandoned the chosen people? Is God as powerful as they'd supposed? And perhaps most profound, why are they suffering? In these chapters the writer spins a stunning new possibility out of the tragedy of the Exile: it's a chance to show the whole world God's redemptive power. In this way the people's suffering becomes a channel for God's salvation, as through them God works to establish a new world order.

The theme of servanthood plays a central role in this radical reframing of the Exile. Again and again the writer calls the faithful exiles, collectively, the "servant" of Yahweh:

> "You are my servant [God says,]
>   I have chosen you and not cast you off."
>   (Isa 41:9)[3]

But how does this identity as *God's servant* fit Isaiah's message of redemption and hope? For one thing, to call the people Yahweh's servant suggests that their God, not Nebuchadnezzar, holds ultimate power. As they lived under house arrest far from home, this was an example of what scholar Anathea E. Portier-Young calls a "radical relocation of ultimate power."[4] When Isaiah calls Yahweh "your Sovereign, the Lord" (Isa 51:22), the writer imagines an alternative universe that tips the balance of power away from foreign overlords and toward God.

But if God holds ultimate power, why do the people suffer? The writer answers this in two ways. On one level the writer explains the *cause* of the Exile as a consequence of the people's sin:

> [The servant Israel] was wounded for our
>   transgressions,
>   crushed for our iniquities. (Isa 53:5)

God has not abandoned them per se, but God has abandoned them to their own devices and desires (see Isa 43:28; 47:6; 50:1).

---

[3] In this section of Isaiah, the word *servant* appears twenty-one times, sixteen of which designate the collective people of Israel (e.g., Isa 41:8; 42:1; 43:19).

[4] See Anathea E. Portier-Young, *Apocalypse against Empire: Theologies of Resistance in Early Judaism* (Grand Rapids, MI: Eerdmans, 2011), 7. Though she's writing about apocalyptic texts, Second Isaiah's use of servanthood fits this description well.

On another level though, Isaiah locates redemptive *meaning* in the Exile, a meaning that reconstitutes the people's personal power in the process. In the midst of their suffering God opens a new way for human flourishing on earth. Of course, it is God who takes the initiative: "See, the Lord God comes with might" (Isa 40:10) and will make a way "in the wilderness" for the people's return to their homeland (Isa 40:3). Yahweh's dramatic intervention in the course of human history, the prophet insists, will convince all the world that "your God reigns" (Isa 52:7).

But this "new way" also engages the servant people as authorized agents of their Lord. Through them—and even in the midst of their powerlessness—God will lay out a global vision for justice and righteousness that renews the earth. What does their part entail? For one thing, God's spirit will work through this servant people (Isa 42:1; 44:3) to declare boldly a message of "justice to the nations" (Isa 42:1; cf. 42:3, 4). As exiles, they may have no power to "cry out or lift up [a] voice" (Isa 42:2); yet God's faithful servant will

> open the eyes that are blind, . . .
> bring out the prisoners from the dungeon,
> > from the prison those who sit in darkness.
> (Isa 42:7)

From the underbelly of oppression God's people will wield a subversive power by announcing and enacting God's counter-cultural, life-giving kingdom.

It's important to note, too, that this servant does not play the victim even when facing the most dehumanizing of tactics. In a bold and deliberate act the servant wields personal power by seizing agency from torturers:

> I gave my back to those who struck me,
> > and my cheeks to those who pulled out the beard. (Isa 50:6)

Confident that the God "who vindicates me is near" (Isa 50:8), the servant strengthens its resolve, setting "face like flint" and declaring, "I shall not be put to shame" (Isa 50:7). For this servant, it's utter trust in God—not in self or in the oppressor—that proves essential to remaining human.

Scholars think the final Servant Song (Isa 52:13—53:12) was especially helpful for early Christians trying to grasp the saving power of a crucified messiah. This passage features a servant who suffers not for his own wrongdoing but for the sin of others. It's a case of collective punishment in two respects: at one level the servant "takes the fall" for the people's sin; at another level the servant serves as collective stand-in for an entire group. Understood this way, this righteous sufferer represents those faithful exiles who bear the brunt of their forebears' unfaithfulness.

If the servant suffers without just cause, it's not a meaningless fate. For Isaiah, neither the suffering nor the infidelity that led to it is the end of the story. Instead, the passage transforms victimhood into a pattern of servant power: by "pouring out himself to death" (Isa 53:12), the servant's self-offering leads the way "out of . . . anguish" and into the light in which "the righteous one, my servant, shall make many righteous" (Isa 53:11). Isaiah thus rewrites the tragic script of the Exile to find redemption through sacrificial servanthood. Out of calamity Isaiah issues a call not to passive victimhood but to the kind of active servanthood that sweeps us up in God's liberating power (Isa 42:6; 49:6).

Redemptive Sacrifice in Second Maccabees and Daniel

If Isaiah recasts servanthood into a model for redemptive power, two texts written during the Syrian occupation interpret willing sacrifice as subversive resistance with liberating effects. Second Maccabees and Daniel advocate different responses to Syrian oppression—from armed uprising to a resolute trust that God will soon sort things out. But both see God at work in the people's suffering; both think those who remain allied with God—and die for that allegiance—become agents in God's liberation of their people, and indeed the whole world; both locate personal power not in saving life at all cost but in offering it in service to God's redemptive regime.

Second Maccabees chronicles both the Syrians' oppressive tactics and the insurgency waged by the faithful. In one account a Syrian official requires the high priest Eleazar to abandon his dietary laws and eat forbidden food or face immediate death. When Eleazar refuses, the writer interprets his deliberate sacrifice in these terms: "So in this way he died, leaving in his death an example of nobility and a memorial of courage, not only to the young but to the great body of his nation" (2 Macc 6:31). His sacrifice models precisely the kind of covenant fidelity the Syrians are out to eliminate. Eleazar offers himself both to God and as an example for those who refuse to abandon allegiance to God, even under threat of death.

In the next chapter a story of seven faithful brothers stakes an even greater claim for the redemptive power of their sacrifice. Like Eleazar, these brothers defy imperial laws intended to "de-create" the occupied people, depriving them of sacred traditions that lie at the heart of their shared identity.[5] Yet, as one brother explains:

> "I, like my brothers, give up my body and life for the laws of our ancestors, appealing to God to show mercy soon to our nation and by trials and plagues to make you confess that he alone is God, and through me and my brothers to bring an end to the wrath of the Almighty that has justly fallen on our whole nation." (2 Macc 7:37–38)

Notice that, like Isaiah's servant, the brothers suffer collective punishment (discipline) meted out by God, not Antiochus (see

---

[5] Ibid. As Portier-Young puts it, "Judea's de-creation paved the way for empire's re-creation" (210).

also 2 Macc 7:12–17). Like Isaiah's servant, this brother belies Syrian power through the willing sacrifice of "body and life." And like Isaiah's servant, the righteous brothers' self-offering bears witness to God's power and helps to save "our whole nation."

Daniel responds to the Syrian occupation by casting sociopolitical reality in an apocalyptic light. For this writer, it's part of a spiritual battle that will lead to God's dominion on the earth. Daniel, too, sees suffering partly as a result of the people's sin (see Dan 9:1–19). It's also a byproduct of the conflict between good and evil playing out in real time: evil lashes out all the more viciously when the end is near. For Daniel, that makes suffering a penultimate circumstance, not an ultimate one. It's the long view that will prevail when "at that time, your people shall be delivered" (Dan 12:1). Then, the faithful shall "shine like the brightness of the sky, and those who lead many to righteousness, like the stars forever and ever" (Dan 12:3). Those who suffer willingly for the cause of God's kingdom participate in the renovation of earth as a beacon of righteousness. Their self-offering is not in vain; instead, it carries redemptive power.

Together, these texts help to frame our view of sacrificial servanthood in Jesus's story. During both the Exile and the Syrian occupation those who called Yahweh "Lord" suffered under power deployed for destructive and violent purposes. Yet faithful writers offer subversively creative glimpses of personal power in the midst of suffering through the pattern of sacrificial servanthood.

SACRIFICIAL SERVANTHOOD IN JESUS'S STORY: AN EMBODIED EXAMPLE

As we've seen, Jesus's death on a Roman cross came not as a surprising departure from his earthly career but as its likely outcome. This is true, too, with the pattern of sacrificial servanthood.

Long before he arrived in Jerusalem, Jesus operated on this counter-cultural power principle, and he invited others to do the same. Gospel accounts of his earthly mission portray Jesus as God's servant who forfeits self-interest to advance God's redemptive dream for the world. As he sets "his face toward Jerusalem" (Luke 10:51), this way of sacrificial servanthood only comes more fully to light.

Jesus in and around Galilee

Jesus's pattern of sacrificial servanthood appears throughout the gospel story, but it sometimes does so in subtle ways. For one thing, readers frequently overlook just how little interest Jesus has in his own celebrity status; in fact, he often actively resists those who would broadcast his identity or power. Mark says that Jesus "would not permit the demons to speak, because he knew them" (Mark 1:34). Even when Peter correctly calls him messiah, Jesus "sternly ordered [the disciples] not to tell anyone about him" (Mark 8:29). Matthew explains Jesus's reticent insistence "not to make him known" (Matt 12:16) by paraphrasing the Servant Song found in Isaiah 42:

> He will not wrangle or cry aloud,
> nor will anyone hear his voice in the
> streets. (Matt 12:19)

Even John's Gospel, which shows more interest in Jesus's divine status than the others, stresses that Jesus's power comes from God. Jesus makes a point of noting that "the Son can do nothing on his own, but only what he sees the Father doing" (John 5:19). The very purpose behind his coming "down from heaven" (John 6:38), Jesus says, is to do "the will of [God] who sent me" (John 4:34; 5:30; 6:38). Here, too, Jesus appears as God's servant, one whose only authority comes not from himself but from his God. Likewise, he exercises that power in a strange way—not by insisting on his own status but by offering himself to the wider purposes of God's will. Ultimately, even Jesus's own glory comes from God and extends, through him, to the faithful community (see John 17:22; cf. Isa 42:6; 49:6).

As God's servant, Jesus sometimes sacrifices personal plans to serve God's purposes. The Gospels preserve intriguing glimpses of just this kind of self-offering in the face of human need. Mark's version of the feeding of the five thousand, for example, portrays Jesus as a reluctant miracle worker who models and involves others in this pattern of sacrificial servanthood. Mark sets the scene when Jesus urges his disciples to "come away to a deserted place all by yourselves and rest a while" (Mark 6:31). Just back from a highly successful venture (see Mark 6:7–13), Jesus implies that the disciples have earned a reprieve (see also Mark 1:35; 6:46). At their intended place of retreat, though, the group finds not solitude but thousands of people who've anticipated their next move. Jesus switches gears, addressing the spiritual hunger of these "sheep without a shepherd" by teaching them "many things" (Mark 6:34).

But there's another shift in the story that captures a snapshot of sacrificial servanthood. As the sun begins to set, the disciples recognize the crowd's physical hunger and propose a reasonable solution: "Send them away so that they may . . . buy something for themselves to eat" (Mark 6:36). Jesus pivots yet again, shifting from spiritual to physical provision—or rather, he commands the disciples to do so: "You give them something to eat" (Mark 6:37). As servants in God's abundant kingdom (see Isa 55:1–2), they offer what little they have so that, with Jesus's help, the guests are satisfied beyond measure. As God's servants, both Jesus and his disciples wait on the hungry crowd, using their sacrifice to bring life.

Other gospel passages promote the saving power of sacrificial servanthood in more explicit ways. After Jesus predicts his destiny for a third time in Mark, James and John skip right past the cross to make this request: "Let us sit, one at your right hand and one at your left, in your glory" (Mark 10:37; cf. Matt 20:21). Grasping for personal power in eternity, Jesus's friends can almost see their lavish thrones in heaven. But Jesus says they've missed his point about personal power: his "glory" comes *through* his suffering, not *in spite of* it.

To explain, Jesus first points out that his "cup" of suffering is theirs to share as well (Mark 10:39). But he also goes on to interpret that suffering as part of his—and their—servant power. Like a good teacher, he sets up an unmistakable contrast between conventional, "Gentile" power and the kind of servant power that befits loyalists to God's kingdom. "You know," he says, "that among the nations (or "Gentiles," Greek: *ethnē*) those who are their *apparent rulers* lord it over *them*, and their great ones are tyrants *over them*" (Mark 10:42, AT). The saying itself makes three suggestive claims about the nature of Gentile power. For one thing, Jesus calls the rulers "supposed" or "apparent" rulers; that is, even the occupying armies' power is illusory and provisional. For another thing, Gentile power is "top-down" power that exerts force from above. Perhaps most subtly, Jesus signals to his disciples that they are not subject to these so-called rulers but to God; Gentile rulers, he says, are tyrants "over them" (not "over you").

This last distinction gets to the nub of the passage: "it is not so among you" (Mark 10:43). Their devotion to God, not Caesar, not only frees them from subjection to Rome, but it also imbues them with a different kind of power. It's a power unleashed when they clamor for status found not at the top but on the bottom of the social order. It's a power that rules from the underside of things, where it serves rather than tyrannizes. "Whoever wishes to become great among you must be your servant," he says, "and whoever wishes to be first among you must be slave of all" (Mark 10:43–44). Jesus affirms their aspiration to greatness, but he redefines greatness in terms of servanthood.

Of course, this call to servanthood takes its cues from Jesus's own mission and purpose. Jesus explains the pattern of sacrificial servanthood this way: "For the Son of Man came not to be served but *to serve*, and to *give his life* a ransom for many" (Mark 10:45, emphasis added). Who is this Son of Man, sometimes called the "Human One"? Within this passage Jesus seems to refer to his own mission in the world. But in Jesus's setting, the term also pointed beyond an individual figure toward the "new humanity" this "Human One" establishes. Jesus is the "Human One" in the Gospels because he is just this kind of prototype—the "firstborn of all creation" (Col 1:15), as one writer puts it. As a result, *his* pattern of servanthood sets the terms for his disciples' power; *his* sacrifice means that they too will "give themselves" to his cause.

What's the ransom Jesus's sacrificial servanthood secures? Perhaps this passage implies that Jesus frees those, like James and John, who remain captive to status and power in the conventional sense. Perhaps Jesus gives his life to set us free from pretentious self-interest that locates personal power in lofty delusions of grandeur. Perhaps Jesus liberates us from stifling self-interest so that we, too, come not to be served but to serve, and to give our lives to help set others free.

Jesus in Jerusalem

Jesus's way of sacrificial servanthood ultimately leads him to Jerusalem and the cross that awaits him there. Scholars think the evangelists tell the Passion story in ways that emphasize this theme. By connecting Jesus's death to Isaiah's servant, they lay claim to the redemptive patterns found in that sacred tradition. Thus he appears not as Rome's victim but as God's servant, whose sacrifice brings new life.

Yet even before the Passion, Jesus's final days include episodes that apply this pattern of sacrificial servanthood to those aligned, through him, with God's kingdom. Notably, two women exemplify the kind of personal power that comes from self-offering. One, a poor widow, places two small copper coins in the Temple treasury, a gift that surpasses the "large sums" donated by the wealthy. How could this be? Jesus explains the contrast: "For all of them have contributed out of their abundance; but she out of her poverty has put in everything she had, *her very life*" (Mark 12:44, AT; cf. Luke 21:4). It's the sacrificial dimension of her contribution, in contrast with the token gift of the wealthy, that constitutes the offering of "all she had to live on," that is, her very life. No one compelled her; she acted as a free agent. No one—apart from Jesus—even recognized her act; she gave her very being to her God not to curry anyone's favor but out of utter devotion to God.

Another nameless woman goes to great expense to anoint Jesus as the Christ. When she breaks a costly alabaster jar, some question the prudence of her lavish act. But Jesus rises to her defense with these words: "What she had, she did: she has anointed my body ahead of time for burial" (Mark 14:8, AT; cf. Matt 26:12). Even more, he predicts that this act of sacrifice becomes part and parcel of the "good news," so that wherever it's proclaimed "in the whole world, what she has done will be told in remembrance of her" (Mark 14:9). In each case the woman's sacrificial act reveals a personal power that willingly invests itself in God's life-giving reign. By nature, this kind of sacrifice isn't coerced; it doesn't secure worldly glory or inflict harm on others. It's a deliberate and sacrificial act of devotion to God and God's saving power. And it turns out that it saves them in the process.

Jesus's last evening with his disciples draws the saving power of sacrificial servanthood into focus. Though their stories differ in the details, the Gospels all assign momentous staying power to Jesus's symbolic acts that night. The Synoptic writers describe a Passover meal that soon becomes foundational for early Christian gatherings. In Mark's telling, Jesus first offers a loaf of bread, which he calls "my body" (Mark 14:22), and then shares a cup that represents the "blood of the covenant, which is poured out for many" (Mark 14:24). Together, these simple elements represent Jesus's sacrificial self-offering. Like the martyred brother in Second Maccabees, Jesus willingly forfeits flesh and blood as his devotion to the one God leads him into the deathly snares of imperial power. He faces his death, then, not as an isolated radical but as one who thinks his deliberate sacrifice will bring release "for many."

John's Gospel offers another version of this final gathering, but it too features Jesus's example of sacrificial servanthood. In John, there's no mention of a meal; instead, Jesus takes a servant's posture as he prepares to wash his disciples' feet. Though Peter protests, Jesus insists it's essential to having a "share with me" (John 13:8). But that "share" entails more than receiving Jesus's act of sacrificial service; it also means performing it toward others. Jesus explains it this way:

> For I have set you an example, that you also should do as I have done to you. Very truly, I tell you, servants are not greater than their master, nor are messengers greater than the one who sent them. (John 13:15–16)

Just as Jesus's servant act grows out of his obedience to God ("the one who sent" him), so too does he model that servanthood for those whom he sends out to carry forward his messianic mission.

Following this private encounter with his disciples—which extends in John for five chapters—the group makes its way to the Mount of Olives. It's there, in the Garden of Gethsemane, that Jesus most explicitly submits his own inclinations to God's redemptive purposes. Again, the Gospels tell the story differently, sometimes toning down Jesus's anguish as he faces impending doom. As the earliest account, Mark's story is most poignant; there, Jesus twice asks God to "remove this cup from me" (Mark 14:36, 39). Yet he finally relents, uttering "not what I will, but what you want" (Mark 14:36). From this point in the story his resolve strengthens as he faces his betrayer, his arrest, and his death with the quiet purpose reminiscent of Isaiah's servant.

In all these ways the Gospels agree that Jesus's earthly mission and his death on a Roman cross embody the saving power of sacrificial servanthood. As God's servant, Jesus is no mere victim but willingly offers up "all that he had"—even his very life—in service to a new world order of redemption and release. In this sense, too, his sacrificial death redeems personal power from fearful captivity to self-concern. In this way Jesus's sacrificial servanthood makes a "way in the wilderness" that leads to abundant life.

THE WAY OF THE CROSS: FROM SELF-INTEREST TO SELF-SACRIFICE

We've seen that sacrificial servanthood is part of Jesus's story from start to finish. Even in the Gospels that redemptive pattern applies not just to him, but to those who'd "take up a cross and follow." And it's in this pattern that we see "true power" that Rutledge describes this way:

> True power is best seen in a life willingly offered as sacrifice *for the sake of others*. There is unexcelled strength in such sacrifice when it is embraced—not simply imposed or inflicted—as a way of aligning oneself with the good kind of power (emphasis added).[6]

This power doesn't detour around suffering but plods headlong through it. It turns on end conventional power that shows up as coercive force, even force justified as self-protection. It also subverts notions of personal power attached to social or religious or economic status secured through strategies of self-promotion. Instead, the cross models self-offering "for the sake of others"—that is, in service to God's renewal of the earth.

---

[6] Fleming Rutledge, *The Crucifixion: Understanding the Death of Jesus Christ* (Grand Rapids, MI: Eerdmans, 2015), 274.

Outside the Gospels, other early Christian writers highlight this dimension of the cross's saving power. For the apostle Paul, Jesus's execution shifted the axis of power from death to life; on the cross, Jesus's willing sacrifice enacted God's decisive defeat of evil. But the saving power of the cross, for Paul, is not just about believing this good news. Rather, his letters consistently call Jesus's followers to imitate this counter-cultural kind of power.

Paul's letter to the Philippians, for instance, incorporates an early Christian hymn to memorialize Jesus's sacrificial death *as a way of life*. Paul wants his audience to build a unified front as agents of God's redemption. To that end, he implores them to "do nothing from selfish ambition or conceit" and to "look not to your own interests, but to the interests of others" (Phil 2:3, 4). But more than just urging them to "play nice," Paul anchors this encouragement in the sacrificial pattern of Jesus's death.

Let the same mind be in you that was in Christ Jesus,

> who, though he was in the form of God,
> did not regard equality with God
> as something to *lead to plunder*,
> but *emptied himself*,
> taking the form of a *servant*,
> being born in human likeness.
> And being found in human form,
> he humbled himself
> and became obedient to the point of
> death—
> even death on a cross (emphasis added).
> (Phil 2:5–8, AT)

What does Jesus's story have to do with the Philippian community? When we "look to the interests of others" (Phil 2:4; 1 Cor 10:24) rather than to our own interests, Paul thinks, we adopt the "mind of Christ" as our dominant framework for living in the world. For Paul, Jesus's death saves us in part by pointing the way to the pattern of sacrificial servanthood.

What are the signposts along this way? The hymn begins by noting Jesus's own starting point: he was "in the form of God." For Paul, God's story of redemption in Christ begins by alluding to the divine imprint that all human beings bear (see Gen 1:27). Even Jesus's "equality with God," though, doesn't bring license for exploitative power; Jesus's personal *and decidedly divine* power emphatically doesn't "become something to be exploited."

Rather than grasping for others' lives or resources, Christ secured power by casting aside his privilege and prestige to become a servant, a loyal ally of the God who gives life. In the ancient world (as in ours), this depiction of divine power as self-emptying, servant-like obedience wasn't the winner in the marketplace of ideas. There, imperial messaging presented Rome's domination as evidence of divine power. Across the Mediterranean, people recognized power in strength, not weakness; dominance, not servitude; violent force, not subjection to it; self-promotion, not self-sacrifice. Yet, for Paul, Jesus's life pattern of self-emptying or self-denial put God's alternative, and redemptive, power structure on bold display.

The Philippians must have grappled with such notions of personal power. Scholars think Paul's communities were made up of those from a wide range of social, ethnic, and religious backgrounds. They entered this messianic movement with a clear sense of where they were in the pecking order. They brought to it the human impulse to assert their views, preferences, and interests over and against those of others. Paul asks them—implores them, really—to set aside self-interest and locate personal power elsewhere, namely in self-emptying devotion to God. In this move, he thinks, the saving power of Jesus's death begins to take root.

Paul makes a similar point when he writes to the Corinthians about their table manners (1 Cor 11:17–34). In the ancient world, meal practices represented a microcosm of the wider social order. The Corinthians, it seems, had departed from their host culture by gathering to eat in "mixed company." But they hadn't gone all the way, in Paul's view. The problem he diagnoses is that when they gather, "one goes hungry and another becomes drunk" (1 Cor 11:21). Paul's dismay at such stratification is palpable: this is *not*, he says, "the Lord's supper" (1 Cor 11:20). Though Corinthian society would have taken this inequality for granted, Paul thought those who call Jesus "Lord" should not. Their allegiance to the "unimperial empire" established by this messiah named Jesus means that those with more resources should share with those who have less. And he's miffed that they've missed the memo.

As in Philippians, Paul appeals to Jesus's story to support his point. What does "the Lord's supper" look like? Paul reminds the Corinthians about Jesus's own table manners in the last meal shared with his disciples. He carefully crafts Jesus's words to emphasize Jesus's self-sacrifice: "This *of me* is the body, the one *for you*" (1 Cor 11:24, AT). To "do *this* in remembrance of me," then, is to honor Jesus's sacrifice by taking what's "mine" (literally "of me") and giving it up "for you"—that is, for those who are hungry. Paul's worried about more than proper protocol for worship; he's reminding the Corinthians of Jesus's sacrificial servanthood, seen in the cross as well as throughout his career. Those who follow Jesus as their Lord, he insists, will bear witness to the personal and social power unleashed when self-interest gives way to self-offering. For Paul, it's a matter of life and death (1 Cor 11:30).

The writer of Hebrews also uses the theme of sacrifice to explain the saving significance of Christ's death. There, Jesus takes on the role of "great high priest" who has "once for all … put away sin by the sacrifice of himself" (Heb 9:26; cf. 7:27; 9:12; 10:10). By merging his will with God's (Heb 10:6), Jesus has become the "pioneer and perfecter of our faith" (Heb 12:2). Yet even in Hebrews, Jesus's game-changing, redemptive death incorporates his followers in the new world order he's established. After all, they too have "endured a hard struggle with sufferings" and "cheerfully accepted the plundering of . . . possessions" (Heb 10:32, 34); the writer enjoins them too to "do good and to share what you have, for such sacrifices are pleasing to God" (Heb 13:16). Christ has opened the way of faith to them, a way that's marked by saving sacrifice that has "once for all" charted a course for sacrificial allegiance to God.

CONCLUDING THOUGHTS

In Christian teaching some have defined sin as the "soul turned inward upon itself." This impulse to preserve, protect, and defend ourselves and our resources at any cost is a deeply human one that the first-century world openly encouraged. In that context, personal power had much to do with one's social, economic, and even physical strength. In turn, those who wanted to enhance that power saw nothing wrong with insisting on their own advantage over others, often to the point of exploitation and violence.

Into this context stepped a "lord" whose sovereign power belonged to a new world order. As Jesus modeled the way of sacrificial servanthood, he forfeited his own privileged status in service to God's kingdom, a kingdom that exerted power from the bottom up. In his call to "deny oneself and take up the cross," he invited others to do the same—that is, to reframe personal power in terms of giving not getting, of serving not being served.

As it redeems self-interest through self-sacrifice, this way of the cross is no call to self-inflicted harm—physical, emotional, or spiritual. Nor is it a call to resignation, victimhood, or self-loathing. It is not, as Darwish discovered, a call to martyrdom in the conventional sense. We cannot state this point emphatically enough. Instead, to deny oneself is to serve willingly as an agent of redemptive power that's loose in the world.

This call to "take up the cross" speaks to people of faith across the social and economic spectrum. For those of us who enjoy positions of social and economic strength, the way of sacrificial servanthood makes us downwardly mobile. To "lose ourselves" means loosening our grip on power secured by grasping at things and exploiting those beneath us. But it goes beyond that. It means giving our "whole life" as an act of what John Howard Yoder calls "revolutionary subordination." As those accustomed to being in charge, we set aside self-interest as our guiding principle as we join in God's redemptive dream for the world. The cost for such a journey can be steep; letting go of our privilege and comfort and acclaim is no easy task. Just ask Jesus. But the gospel promise is this: this release from self-concern plugs us into a source of personal power that brings not just life, but life abundant (John 10:10).

The call can be just as challenging for those "people on the cross" who already struggle for every last breath. For them, the way of sacrificial servanthood recasts suffering as a locus for true personal power. Rather than sanctioning or legitimizing that suffering, Jesus's call to "take up the cross" willingly transforms victimhood into agency and weakness into strength. It's a different way of fighting back, with a different kind of personal power. It's a power that comes not from hunkering down or lashing out, but from freely entrusting the whole self to the grace of God's redemptive ways.

But let's face it. Regardless of our station in life, all of us at times feel utterly powerless—in a relationship, in the workplace, in the chaos of our wider world. Regardless of our station in life, all of us have opportunities to exert crippling power. That's why it's so important to be clear about what *kind* of personal power Jesus's death embodies. It's a power that comes when we wake up to the truth that we are not our own. It's the "unexcelled strength," as Rutledge puts it, we find when we let ourselves be absorbed in God's mysterious plan to save us all from what King calls the "permanent death of the spirit." It's the freedom unleashed when, by grace, we begin to loosen the grip on our fragile, protective selves, one clenched finger at a time.

7

The Cross, God, and the Unexpected Places

Mitri Raheb

By their very nature, empires raise the question about God. They behave like God: they're omnipotent; they produce, own, and operate the latest inventions in military sophistication; they can dictate their conditions and no one can object. In a victorious and mocking tone they pose the question to those they conquer: "Where is your God?" (Ps 42:10).

People feeling the heat of the empire, its oppression, its occupation, its military power, can't help but pass the question on to heaven, asking, "God, where are you?" It's a three thousand-year-old lament inhabitants of Palestine—Jewish, Christian, and Muslim—have passed on from one generation to the next. It is a question that echoes throughout the Bible. It is a question of a people whose faith is continually tested. They question neither the existence of God nor his care, but they do wonder why God is not moving. He sees his people being oppressed, He knows how they are being treated, and yet he seems to be so silent. The cry is supposed to shake him so that he awakes, acts, and delivers.

Excerpts from this chapter were published in Mitri Raheb, *Faith in the Face of Empire: The Bible through Palestinian Eyes* (Maryknoll, NY: Orbis Books, 2014), 67–69.

I've lived under Israeli occupation almost all of my life, going through ten wars in less than fifty-five years. I've seen people work hard to build homes and lives only to see them repeatedly destroyed; I've seen dreams suffocating under the Israeli occupation. I can't help but ask once more, "God, where are you?"

Yet throughout the Bible—with the exception of the Exodus—the God in whom the people of Palestine put their faith appears to be silent. He sees the Assyrians resettling his people and does nothing; he watches the Babylonians desecrate his temple, and he doesn't move an inch; his capital is destroyed by the Romans, and he appears not to care. Even when his only beloved Son hangs on the cross, he is *absconditus*; more than absent, God seems almost in hiding.

This has been the experience of the people of Palestine throughout history, regardless of religious affiliation. In 614 CE, when the Persians destroyed over three thousand churches in Palestine and left little save the Church of the Nativity, God did nothing to push the invaders back. When the Crusaders plundered churches in the Holy Land, God did not lift a finger. When Palestinians were driven out of their homes in 1948 in what we call the Nakbah (Catastrophe), God was silent. When the Church of the Nativity was besieged in 2002, God did not interfere. And as tens of thousands of Christians flee the Middle East for their lives today, neither God nor the so-called Christian world seems to do anything. The God in whom the people of Palestine put their faith seems to be weak and not up to the challenge. Like his people, he appears to have neither the means nor the resources to confront the occupying empires. And so the old question still echoes today, "God, where are you?"

It is not by chance that the divine revelation took place in Palestine. The revelation wasn't the notion that *there is a God* somewhere and after all, but biblical revelation was the response to that perennial question, "Where are you, God?" The people of Palestine, our forefathers and foremothers, discovered a unique and surprising answer, and the response to it made history.

Of course, some thought God was visible and omnipresent in grand shrines and temples that glorified both God and empire. The God of the empire was as omnipotent as the empire. Indeed, his power and that of the empire were almost interchangeable. He was a victorious God—the perfect match for a victorious empire.

On the other hand, there was the God of the people of Palestine, whose tiny territory resembled a corridor in Middle Eastern geography. His country lacked resources and power. Above all, this God appeared to be weak compared with other gods. He seemed forever to be on the losing end, just like his people. This God, too, was almost interchangeable with his people; his weakness was shown in theirs; and their defeat was his. This God was a loser. He lost almost all wars, and his people paid the price of those defeats. In short, God did not appear to be up to the challenge of the various occupying empires.

But the people of Palestine received a revelation that enabled them to spot God where no one else could see him, and to find him in the most unexpected places. When his people were driven as slaves into Babylon, they witnessed him packing up and accompanying them. When his capital, Jerusalem, was destroyed and his Temple plundered, he appeared to them in the ashes. When his people were defeated, he was also present. The salient feature of this God was that he didn't run away when his people faced their destiny, but remained with them, showing solidarity and choosing to share their destiny.

The climax of the New Testament could not have been anything else but God on the cross. Consequently and ultimately, Jesus revealed none other than this God on the cross, in a situation of terrible agony, and pain, brutally crushed by the empire and hanging like a rebellious freedom fighter. The cross became the ultimate unexpected place for God's revelation. The people of Palestine could then say with great certainty: "For we do not have a high priest who is unable to sympathize with our weak-nesses, but we have one who in every respect has been tested as we are" (Heb 4:15).

For the people of Palestine, the fact that God revealed him-self in the most unexpected place of Palestine meant that defeat in the face of the empire was not an ultimate defeat. It meant that after the country was devastated by the Babylonians, when everything seemed to be lost, a new beginning was possible. Even when the dwelling place of God was destroyed, God survived that destruction, developing in response a dwelling that was indestructible. Ultimately, when Jesus cried on the cross, "My God, my God, why have you forsaken me?" that soul-rending plea was just the prelude to the resurrection (Mark 15:34).

The revelation made in Palestine was that God was to be found in the most unexpected places and where no one expected him. To Gentiles this sounded like "foolishness," and even for Jews it was a "stumbling block." For Paul, such a revelation was nothing less than "the power of God and the wisdom of God" (1 Cor 1:23–24).

This revelation was and is of utmost importance. For it enabled the people of Palestine to survive all defeats. It made the defeat lose its teeth, death lose its sting, and empire lose its victory. It ensured that empires were incapable of celebrating their victories, because while they crushed the people they oc-cupied, they weren't able to crush their spirit.

This is precisely what this revelation did for the people of Palestine. It helped them not to surrender after each defeat, but to pick themselves up and start over again. It made them develop an art of resilience to survive extremist empires, "af-flicted in every way, but not crushed; perplexed, but not driven to despair; persecuted, but not forsaken; struck down, but not destroyed" (2 Cor 4:8–9).

The year 2017 marks the one-hundredth anniversary of the Balfour Declaration, in which the British Empire promised the land of our ancestors to the European Jews as part of a European colonial endeavor. Since that time our land has been undergoing a systemic plan of colonization implemented by the Israeli forces with the blessings of the imperial powers. The year 2017 also marks the fiftieth anniversary of the occupation of the West Bank, the Gaza Strip, and the Golan Heights. I was five years old when I saw Israeli soldiers marching in the little town of Bethlehem. Since then, I've watched what the occupation does to our community. I've seen how the whole West Bank looks more and more like a piece of Swiss cheese, where Israel gets the "cheese"—the land and its resources—and the Palestinians are pushed into the "holes."

I witness this in my own hometown Bethlehem, where 86 percent of our land is not under our control. Instead, it's being colonized by Jewish settlers who exploit our resources, stones, water, and minerals. I follow the building of the wall, equipped with the latest surveillance technology, not on the green line (the border of Palestinian territory, by international law) but in the backyard of the last home in town. As a pastor I see how this occupation is destroying the fabric of our society: a city that can't expand is doomed to die; without possibilities for building new neighborhoods, we can't do any reasonable city planning. The little town is losing its character. With no freedom to build homes or to travel to other parts of the West Bank, unemployment continues to rise. Of course, people without jobs create a climate of social tension, crime, drugs, and violence.

This is not a natural catastrophe that comes from heaven, but a manmade and systematically planned catastrophe that is subsidized partly by the international community. As a pastor who lives in the little town, I keep asking myself how our people will survive—physically, socially, economically, and spiritually. The continuing occupation denies us our freedom and the right to exercise our self-determination. It dehumanizes our people. The occupation not only steals our land, but also our resources and our future and that of our children. It robs them of a life lived with dignity and abundance.

The Israeli military occupation combines three oppressive systems in one in an unholy trinity. It copied the system of reservations from the North American continent, combined it with the apartheid system from South Africa, and added, from East Germany, a separation wall. This creates one of the most oppressive and longest military occupations in modern history.

What is more, the Israeli military uses the occupied territories for live field tests of the latest security products and equipment. And the Israeli economy exploits the natural resources of Palestine and then sells them back, in the form of consumer products. Under these circumstances life becomes unbearable. Estimates are that Gaza will be uninhabitable by the year 2020.

I hear the cry of our people, "Wenak ya Allah?" Where are you, God? How long, O Lord? Why do you allow this to happen? Why isn't there any justice in this world? Even the United Nations gives advantage to world powers with no real care for those who are powerless. And still, God seems not to care about a situation that goes from bad to worse.

One would think that after one hundred years of colonization of Palestine; after the Catastrophe of 1948 and the loss of land; after the occupation of the West Bank and the Gaza Strip in 1967; after two unsuccessful uprisings in 1987 and 2000; after three brutal aggressions on Gaza that brought lots of destruction; after imprisoning hundreds of thousands of Palestinians in Israeli jails without trials; after these series of Palestinian defeats in the face of an Israeli colonial project—one would expect the people of Palestine to surrender, to give up, to admit their ultimate defeat.

Yet nothing of the sort happens. On the contrary, pushed outside of their homeland, a new generation of young Palestinians is helping the movement known as "Boycott, Divestment, Sanctions" (or BDS). They're confronting the monopoly of Israel's lobby on many US university campuses. In Palestine,

those whose homes were demolished by Israeli-operated Cat-
erpillar equipment or F-16s are not surrendering to this power
of destruction. Instead, they simply rebuild their homes and
lives. With all its power and might, the empire can't crush the
spirit of the people of Palestine and thus can't celebrate ultimate
victory. Like the old Judeans who sat on the river of Babylon
and could not forget Jerusalem, so also the Palestinians in the
diaspora today continue to remember Jerusalem, even if they
are not allowed to pay it a visit.

The situation under occupation is very depressing, not only
for Palestinians but for many who care for both Palestine and
Israel and the people who inhabit them. Visitors to Bethlehem
find themselves dismayed as they see the wall on three sides of
the little town and experience the entrenched system of segregation. God seems to be absent from the so-called Holy Land.

But then they tour our ministries, they watch Palestinian
kids dancing with joy in their eyes, Christian and Muslim
girls playing soccer with pride in their faces, students at our
university producing films that tell the human side of our story,
and elderly people writing books sharing their lifelong experiences with the younger generations. They too discover God in
unexpected places.

Palestine was the unexpected place for God to reveal himself. The ultimate revelation on the cross shows that there is no
place on earth, in history, in one's own life, where God cannot
reveal himself. He is there where no one expects him, there
even when we do not count on him, there when hope seems
lost forever. The good news proclaimed on the cross was and
is this: Expect God in the most unexpected places.

8

The Cross and Cosmic Power

The Way of Inclusive Embrace

SUZANNE WATTS HENDERSON

*The world to come is ruled by the one
who on the cross took violence upon himself in order to conquer and embrace
the enemy.*

—MIROSLAV VOLF,
EXCLUSION AND EMBRACE

In this chapter we face head on what may be scripture's boldest
claim. Beyond salvation from political and religious systems
that subjugate and oppress, beyond deliverance from self-
concern, New Testament writers insist that Jesus's death on a
Roman cross has *set the world free from the vice grip of cosmic
evil.* On the cross, they say, Christ has conquered "once and for
all" those forces that threaten the vital flourishing of the whole
created order.

Two thousand years later, of course, it's a claim many
thoughtful Christians quietly doubt or openly deny. With the
people of Palestine, we too might find ourselves asking, "Where
are you, God?" Even if we don't live under a regime that
systematically dismantles our lives and livelihood, we don't

have to look far to find evidence that evil rages in our midst. In our personal lives we know the ravaging power of cancer or addiction, and our relationships with family and friends are sometimes strained to the breaking point. Our communities writhe under the agony of tragic violence, and lines of ethnic, economic, ideological, religious difference seem more deeply drawn with each news cycle. Across the globe people hunker down or flee for their lives from terrorizing force. Even creation itself seems to convulse from the weight of humanity's wanton disregard for the natural world. To say that Jesus's death has defeated cosmic evil can sound naively disconnected from reality, willfully ignorant, or just plain preposterous.

It's easy to forget that the New Testament writers, too, lived in a post-resurrection world where evil ran roughshod over people and their communities. Decades after Christ's death things weren't getting any better; in many instances they were getting worse. Indeed, Christians became an easy if sporadic target for persecution and scapegoating. And still, they insist on such audacious claims as these:

In the world you face persecution. But take courage; I have conquered the world! (John 16:33)

In all these things we are more than conquerors through him who loved us. For I am convinced that neither death, nor life, nor angels, nor rulers, nor things present, nor things to come, nor powers, nor height, nor depth, nor anything else in all creation, will be able to separate us from the love of God in Christ Jesus our Lord. (Rom 8:37–39)

Whatever is born of God conquers the world. And this is the victory that conquers the world, our faith. (1 John 5:4)

Somehow, these writers stand up to the evil of their age emboldened by the "good news" that, on the cross, the "love of God in Christ Jesus" has already won the day. For them, this reconciling love is stronger than death, and those caught in its force field have already become "conquerors."

Is it possible, in our place and time, to recover a robust sense of Christ's decisive victory over evil? Can we live today as "conquerors" who, like Christ, wield not conventional weapons but reconciling love? Can we trust that that love really does win? Let's consider the evidence.

COSMIC POWER
IN CONTEXT

Many scholars think both Jesus and his earliest interpreters saw his life and death as part of an apocalyptic drama.[1] Though the term *apocalyptic* may sound bizarre or off-putting to readers, the worldview it denotes helps us make sense of the cosmic power of the cross. In what follows, we trace key parts of the apocalyptic scheme that New Testament writers both adopt and adapt as they dare to insist that Jesus's death has indeed brought evil to its knees.

> *"O Lord, how long shall I cry for help,*
> *and you will not listen? Or cry to you*
> *'Violence!' and you will not save?"*
>
> (HABAKKUK 1:2)

Jewish apocalyptic voices generally express an urgent sense that things have gone from bad to worse. Though they rarely specify their historical settings, these texts make it clear that cosmic evil seems to have the upper hand. Sometimes, they refer obliquely to

---

[1] This worldview has been coopted and corrupted in popular American fiction and film. Writers like Hal Lindsey (*The Late Great Planet Earth*) and Tim LaHaye (the *Left Behind* series) have profited greatly from "popularizing" the apocalyptic genre, with little regard for its most important biblical elements, which we consider here.

political and military subjugation. But regardless of their specific circumstance, apocalyptic writers see their world at its breaking point under the weight of oppressive strategies that undermine the people's identity and agency. They, too, ask, "Where are you, Lord?"

In essence, Jewish apocalyptic writers address an existential gap between the way things are and the way things ought to be. They see themselves as residents of a "present evil age," an epoch when evil seems to have an upper hand. Notably, they attribute the suffering to more than bad people or policies; as the Qumran Scrolls put it, they're living under the "dominion of Satan/Belial." From this vantage point, evil has invaded the very cosmos and is wreaking havoc among those who suffer the brunt of its brutal, dehumanizing force.

> *"O that you would tear open the heavens*
> *and come down,*
> *so that the mountains would quake at*
> *your presence."*
>
> (ISAIAH 64:1)

This sense of desperation leads to a second feature of apocalyptic thought: a desperate plea for God to reestablish justice on earth, and soon! For these writers, evil is so rampant that the world is beyond human repair. As if imploring a parent to come down and sort things out, these writings both affirm the enduring power of God *in heaven* and wait on tiptoes for its "revelation" (Greek: *apocalypsis*) *on earth*.

As Isaiah's words suggest, apocalyptic writers envision a cosmology in which heaven and earth operate on parallel planes, without much intersection to date. But because they're utterly convinced of God's power in heaven, these texts call on God to penetrate and subdue their own sociopolitical order. They eagerly anticipate the day when, as Daniel's vision puts it,

the [heavenly] court shall sit in judgment,
and [Antiochus's earthly] dominion shall
be taken away,
to be consumed and totally destroyed.
(Dan 7:26)

On that day God's justice will override evil's authority in the earthly realm.

> *"See, the day is coming, burning like an*
> *oven, when all the arrogant and all evildo-*
> *ers will be stubble; . . . But for you who*
> *revere my name the sun of righteousness*
> *shall rise, with healing in its wings."*
> (MALACHI 4:1–2)

In the apocalyptic scheme that justice typically arrives on "the day [of the Lord]," when God wins the battle against evil *for good*. That victory brings with it a "judgment" that sorts competing powers—good from evil, righteous from unrighteous, light from dark. Sometimes, an "anointed" figure (a messiah) presides over this judgment day and pronounces eternal verdicts of salvation and life on the one hand or destruction and death on the other.

This day of reckoning is *good news* for those who suffer under the present world order. Not only will its retributive justice bring a purifying fire to consume the "arrogant and all evildoers"; it will also bring salvation for the righteous from their deathly foes. They look forward to the day when they'll be delivered both from the stranglehold of evil and into a bright future, as they become beacons of God's righteousness ways. Daniel says that the "wise shall shine like the brightness of the sky" (Dan 12:2). Indeed, the whole course of history hinges on this day as the turning point from captivity under the present evil age toward the restoration of "all things" (Rev 21:5).

"For I am about to create new heavens
and a new earth;
the former things shall not be remem-
bered
or come to mind."

(ISAIAH 65:17)

In our own context, popular writers and filmmakers sell their work by stressing the cataclysmic destruction that Armageddon will bring. But apocalyptic writers in Jesus's context mostly put brackets around the suffering, framing it as a penultimate reality that's also preamble to what comes next. For them, apocalyptic conflict leads inexorably to the renewal of the whole cosmos.

In many cases this new creation means nothing less than a radical refurbishment of the created order. Isaiah's vision promises many benefits that will accrue to those who've been saved from the present evil age and delivered into the age to come. Joy erupts from sorrow; life is long and prosperous; even the animal kingdom puts God's peace on display (see Isa 65:17–25). In essence, the world returns to the original state of creation, imbued with goodness, harmony among all creatures, plentiful food, and meaningful days. Put simply, Isaiah says,

They shall not hurt or destroy
on all my holy mountain. (Isa 65:25)

In sum, Jewish apocalyptic writers recast the concussive evil in their midst within a wider, and decidedly hopeful, story: God's redemption of the cosmos. This framework explains dire human suffering as part of an apocalyptic showdown between good and evil. But more important, it looks with full assurance to the "day of the Lord" and the divine justice it will bring. In the meantime, these writers urge their communities to stand their ground in the soil of God's righteous ways. Soon, on the "day of the Lord," they'll find deliverance into life and wholeness and peace.

Despite its sometimes strange features, the apocalyptic worldview includes basic contours that readers today may find quite familiar. We too live in a world where good and evil seem locked in battle. We too sometimes carry a sense of despair, even hopelessness, as things seem to go from bad to worse. We too may urgently look for the day when God's justice will prevail, wholesale. How might Jesus's story—his life, death, and resurrection—help us reclaim hope for our place and time? How might the saving power of the cross be at work in our midst to set things to the right on a cosmic scale? Dare we ask?

COSMIC POWER IN JESUS'S STORY: APOCALYPTIC REMIX

Those who called Jesus the Christ—either in his own lifetime or after the resurrection—believed he'd been anointed by God to play a pivotal part in this apocalyptic drama. In his life, death, and resurrection, gospel writers see evidence that God had indeed torn open the heavens and come down to defeat the forces of death itself. On the cross, they maintain, God has put an end to all that would "hurt or destroy on all my holy mountain" (Isa 65:25).

Jesus's story, then, echoes in many respects the apocalyptic strains we've identified. But the Gospels don't just adopt the scheme wholesale; they adjust it to accommodate the reality before them. These alterations interpret present reality this way: while Christ's death has secured evil's ultimate demise, God continues in the meantime to complete "what is lacking" (Col 1:24) through those who continue to trust in his way of reconciling love. The Gospels thus invite their readers to stand their ground as agents of God's redemption.

Jesus in and around Galilee

Jesus's apocalyptic leanings show up early in the gospel story. For one thing, all four evangelists portray him as successor to an apocalyptic prophet named John the Baptist. This detail is an important one, since it reminds us that Jesus's career as messiah probably grew out of a homegrown renewal movement that looked forward to the coming day of the Lord, when God's forces would roundly defeat the forces of Rome. In both Matthew and Luke, John's message fits well the script described above, as he summons God's wrath upon those who refuse to turn from evil toward righteousness (see Matt 3:1–13; Luke 3:1–17).

It's striking, too, that Jesus probably was baptized by John. This ritual act establishes his own purity, a religious condition required for those who would enter God's kingdom. But it also conveys his utter devotion to that coming kingdom and all it represents. After the baptism, Jesus begins to spread John's message about God's coming reign; like John, he calls others to turn around and trust in it (see Mark 1:14–15; Matt 4:17).

But Jesus also adds his own flourish when he shows that God's heavenly power is *already* taking root on earth, in and through him. When religious leaders accuse him of casting out demons "by the ruler of the demons" (Mark 3:22), Jesus explains his exorcisms this way: "No one can enter a strong man's house and plunder his property without first tying up the strong man; then indeed the house can be plundered" (Mark 3:27). In other words, Jesus combats evil first by restraining Satan. When he heals the sick, calms the sea, casts out demons, or feeds the hungry, Jesus serves as advance agent of God's redemptive power; his mission establishes a foothold for that renewing force even as evil continues to hurt and destroy.

Jesus's teachings also reflect central elements of Jewish apocalyptic thought. For instance, he draws a distinction between those entrusted with the "secret of the kingdom of God" and "those outside, [for whom] everything comes in parables" (Mark 4:11). Such sharp demarcation fits well the apocalyptic notion of insiders and outsiders. And several parables liken God's coming kingdom to an elaborate feast, a standard motif for apocalyptic texts (see, e.g., Matt 22:1–10; Luke 14:16–24). Finally, Jesus frequently alludes to coming judgment, often hailing a coming

Son of Man, literally Son of the Human, who will establish God's reign on earth once and for all (see, e.g., Matt 25:31–45; Mark 13:26–27; cf. Dan 7:13–14). These and other glimpses into Jesus's earthly mission, then, make most sense as a story firmly rooted in the soil of Jewish apocalyptic thought.

Yet Jesus's story also adjusts the apocalyptic script in important ways. These modifications may have begun with Jesus himself. But as decades pass without evidence of cataclysmic judgment, the evangelists continue both to *affirm* and to *adapt* the apocalyptic hope for God's redemption of the world. For instance, Jewish apocalyptic traditions progress on a linear time line, so that the present evil age ends precisely when God arrives "on that day" to mete out justice. But the Gospels alter this time line to create an overlap between the present evil age and the age to come. Though God's power has already broken into the earthly realm, the lion isn't quite yet vegetarian!

To that end, Matthew includes a story about an enemy who sowed "weeds among the wheat" (Matt 13:24–30) in the field where God's kingdom has been planted. When the slaves ask their master what kind of weed-control plan they should employ, he responds, "Let both of them grow together until the harvest," and then the reapers will collect and destroy the weeds (Matt 13:30). In this story Jesus both affirms and delays coming judgment. In the process—and this is key—he discourages judging insider from outsider for the purposes of eradicating the latter (see also Matt 7:1–5; Luke 6:37).

This shift toward the meantime leads to a related adjustment. Jewish apocalyptic writers generally draw indelible lines between good and evil, friend and foe, insider and outsider—all with an eye to annihilating those who stand opposed to God's purposes. And though this dimension doesn't disappear entirely in the Gospels, Jesus's story often blurs the lines, as if to say that the line between good and evil runs through us all. By delivering divine health care to those at the margins, Jesus extends well being beyond tribal boundaries. He touches a leper with healing power and so restores him to his own community

(Mark 1:40–45). After a foreign woman registers a creative plea, he heals her daughter and so reflects the inclusive embrace of the "nations" (or "Gentiles") in God's kingdom (Mark 7:24–30). And John tells the story of a Samaritan woman who finds restorative power in the "living water" Jesus provides (John 4:1–30). In all four Gospels, Jesus extends his inclusive embrace to those considered part of the social and religious opposition.

But it's not just his encounters with outsiders that break down binary distinctions deployed to vilify the opposition. His teachings, too, consistently affirm the radical human dignity of those who belong to the category of "other," *even if they are allied with evil*. This emphasis is perhaps most striking in the Sermon on the Mount found in Matthew (and Luke, with some variation), where Jesus says,

> You have heard that it was said, "Love your neighbor and hate your enemy." But I tell you, love your enemies and pray for those who persecute you, that you may be children of your Father in heaven. He causes his sun to rise on the evil and the good, and sends rain on the righteous and the unrighteous. (Matt 5:43–45; see Luke 6:27–31)

In this passage Jesus reimagines even the enemy as an insider. How does he do this? He sees beyond human distinction into the wider landscape of God's kingdom. There, even those set apart as evil or unrighteous partake in the good care of a gracious God. And if God doesn't discriminate, he suggests, neither should God's "children." The command to "love your enemies and pray for those who persecute you" breaks down human boundaries to extend divine love to all people; it pushes lines marking insider from outsider to the outer reaches of the cosmos. It's a revised apocalyptic scenario in which God's loving power encompasses nothing less than the whole of creation.

Jesus in Jerusalem

Apocalyptic writers typically see Jerusalem as the "ground zero" where divine power will invade the world for good. In many cases Jerusalem (often called Zion) is the "holy mountain" where God's people will so radiate justice and righteousness that "all the nations" (Isa 2:2) be drawn into the aura of God's reign. It's not surprising, then, that the Gospels all depict Jesus's death *in Jerusalem* as the moment when God acted decisively to release the world from death itself.

We've seen that Jesus's entry into Jerusalem carried weighty political and religious implications; indeed, he probably created enough of a stir to merit close watch by the authorities. But it's important to note the apocalyptic tenor of that prophetic act. In Zechariah the "king comes to you . . . humble, and riding on a donkey" (Zech 9:9). But the passage announces more than regime change in conventional, earthly terms. It's the dawn of God's cosmic reign upon the earth, a dominion that "shall be from sea to sea, and from the River to the ends of the earth" (Zech 9:10). In other words, Jesus's donkey ride goes way beyond inciting an insurgency that will replace one human kingdom with another; it heralds a new world order in which God's sovereign power encompasses all of creation.

Jesus's apocalyptic leanings come clearly into view when he sees through the impressive Herodian Temple structure to the fragility of the present world order. In his mission, he thinks, the apocalyptic scheme has been set in motion so that

> when you hear of wars and rumors of wars, do not be alarmed; this must take place, but the end is still to come. . . . This is but the beginning of the birth pangs." (Mark 13:7–8; cf. Matt 24:6–7; Luke 21:9–11).

In the Gospels this passage reassures post-resurrection readers that conflict with evil remains an inevitable part of this unfolding drama; it also promises that "the one who endures to the end will be saved" (Mark 13:14). Thus this apocalyptic teaching brings a word of hope by stressing that suffering in the present gives way in the end to deliverance and life.

When religious leaders interrogate him, too, Jesus leaves little doubt that he locates his own story within an unfolding apocalyptic drama. As we've seen, he answers the question about his identity by pointing to signs of the messianic age:

> "You will see the Son of Man
> seated at the right hand of the Power,"
> and "coming with the clouds of heaven."
>   (Mark 14:62; cf. Dan 7:13–14)

Whether these traditions come from Jesus or his interpreters, they see his death as a pivotal event that will bring the Son of Man to earth to preside over the coming "day of the Lord." It's no wonder, then, that those aligned with the present world order find this prediction dangerous.

The Synoptic Gospels put a particularly apocalyptic spin on Jesus's death. Mark says that just after Jesus's last breath, "the curtain of the temple was torn in two, from top to bottom" (Mark 15:37; see Matt 27:51; cf. Luke 23:45). In the Temple's inner sanctum a veil separated God's seat (often called the Holy of Holies) from the surrounding space, indicating a clear boundary between sacred and profane. With Jesus's death, Mark implies, God has heard Isaiah's cry to "tear open the heavens and come down" (Isa 64:1); on the cross, God's defeat of evil means that the divine presence now roams free throughout creation. Jesus's death brings an apocalypse ("unveiling" or "revelation") of the cosmic power of divine love. Matthew amplifies this point by adding details that are standard fare in apocalyptic texts: "The earth shook, and the rocks were split. The tombs also were opened, and many bodies of the saints who had fallen asleep were raised" (Matt 27:51–52). In other words, Jesus's death releases God's life force, which delivers even the dead to new life.

As the latest Gospel, John is the least apocalyptic, at least in the conventional sense. Here, Jesus mentions God's kingdom rarely, and when he does, the concept has taken on a decidedly spiritual sense. (Those who equate the kingdom of God with heaven take their cues mostly from John.) One example appears in John's Passion story, when Pilate asks Jesus if he's the "King of the Jews." Jesus replies, "My kingdom is not of this world" (John 18:36).

But John does preserve the apocalyptic sense that Jesus's death brings God's cosmic defeat of evil. Like the other evangelists, John tinkers with the time frame—only more so. In John's Gospel judgment comes not at some endtime court scene but in Jesus's earthly mission: "*Now* is the judgment of this world; *now* the ruler of this world will be driven out. And I, when I am lifted up from the earth, will draw all people to myself" (John 12:31–32, emphasis added). Not only has judgment day already dawned in Jesus's ministry, but his death clearly brings the demise of the "ruler of this world" *through his inclusive embrace of all people.* In Christ, God's power has penetrated the created order for the purposes of reconciling "all people to myself."

Elsewhere, John emphasizes Jesus's cosmic power in life and in death. In his "Farewell Discourse" (John 13—17), Jesus explains his coming death this way:

> I will no longer talk much with you, for the *ruler of this world* [Greek: *kosmos*] is coming. He has no power over me; but I do as the Father has commanded, so that the world may know that I love the Father. (John 14:30–31, emphasis added)

As in Jewish apocalyptic thought, Jesus sees the "ruler of this world" (Satan) as the cosmic force that God *allows* to operate in the meantime. Satan has "no power," Jesus suggests, because all power really belongs to the Father. For Jesus, even evil remains under God's sway. That's why, on the cross, John's

134 The Cross in Contexts

Jesus utters these words: "It is finished" (John 19:30). It's as if the whole purpose of his coming into the world has been to die.

And in some respects this is true. After all, early in the Gospel, Jesus says, "Just as Moses lifted up the serpent in the wilderness, so must the Son of Man be lifted up, that whoever trusts in him may have eternal life" (John 3:14–15). In the Torah, Moses "lifts up" a serpent both as emblem of the people's sin and as a source of their healing and life (see Num 21:4–9). In a similar way Jesus's death discloses the full measure of endemic evil even as it dispenses the antidote.

What is that antidote? For John, it's the reconciling power of divine love. After all, God's *love* first stirred the impulse to send the son into the world, "not to condemn the world [*cosmos*] but in order that the world might be saved through him" (John 3:16–17). While this plan clearly includes individual salvation, it's also more ambitious than that. Jesus comes *so that the very cosmos will be saved* through him.

Of course, God's reconciling love is the calling card of Jesus's power in John: "Love one another *as I have loved you,*" he teaches his disciples (John 15:12, emphasis added). It becomes, too, the calling card for the community he leaves behind, so that "everyone will know that you are my disciples, if you have love for one another" (John 13:35). Their love, Jesus prays, will be the same "love with which [*God has*] loved me" (John 17:26, AT)—that is, a love that overwhelms creation for God's cause. It is this love, laid bare on the cross, that draws "all people" into the life-giving power of God.

Though the Gospels speak to a world convulsing under evil's power, they all insist that on the cross the axis of power had tilted away from deathly force and toward divine, reconciling love. Even before his resurrection Jesus's death signified for them that the battle had been won, that God's life-giving power had begun to renew the whole cosmos. On the cross God's inclusive embrace had set the world free from death and shown the way, once and for all, to life and hope.

THE WAY OF THE CROSS:
FROM OPPOSITION TO RECONCILING LOVE

Outside the Gospels, other New Testament writers insist that Christ's death has secured God's cosmic victory over evil. Like the evangelists, they too speak a word of hope into a meantime reality marked by human deprivation and despair; they too see *through* the evidence of the present evil age to affirm that, on the cross, the forces of death have met their match. How do they detect God's cosmic victory while creation still groans "in labor pains until now" (Rom 8:22)? And what difference does that victory make in the meantime?

In many ways these questions lie at the heart of Paul's writings. The apostle himself was probably an apocalyptic Jew before a "revelation" (Gal 1:16) convinced him that the crucified Jesus was indeed God's anointed one. For him, as for all Jews, that revelation required quite a conceptual leap, since the messianic age begun in Christ did not yet fit traditional hopes for a peaceable kingdom. Yet like the Gospels—and even before them—Paul adapts the apocalyptic scheme to establish a meantime between what he calls "the ends of the ages" (1 Cor 10:11). Convinced that the cross has already disclosed the very "power of God" (1 Cor 1:18), Paul also awaits the "end" when Christ will "put all enemies under his feet" (1 Cor 15:25).

More than end-time beliefs, though, it's how his communities *live together in the present* that matters most to Paul. And how they live, he thinks, depends on where their allegiances lie: will they join forces with the present evil age and its minions of death, or will they live as "children of God" who play a vital part in the "ministry of reconciliation" (2 Cor 5:18) that Christ's death has begun? What does that "ministry of reconciliation" look like?

For one thing, it means breaking down ethnic and religious lines that divide one from another. This is a live issue in Galatians, where Paul engages in vigorous debate with those who require non-Jewish members of the churches to observe Torah's boundary markers. Paul blames such division not only on bad policy or incorrect doctrine but on what he calls "elemental spirits" (Greek: *stoicheia*), a force associated with the present evil age. For those called to live as if God's reconciling power has broken through, such rules no longer serve their purpose. Paul puts it bluntly: "For neither circumcision nor uncircumcision is anything; but a new creation is everything!" (Gal 6:15). In Christ's death God has created a world in which, Paul says, "There is no longer Jew or Greek, there is no longer slave or free, there is no longer male and female; for all of you are one in Christ" (Gal 3:28).

In what's probably his last letter Paul offers apocalyptic hope for those living under the shadow of the present evil age in Rome. While he acknowledges their suffering, he reframes it within the scope of God's loving embrace. "Who will separate us from the love of Christ?" he asks. "Will hardship, or distress, or persecution, or famine, or nakedness, or peril, or sword?" The answer is emphatic: "No, *in all these things*, we are more than conquerors through him who loved us" (Rom 8:35, 37, emphasis added). The victory secured in Christ's loving, reconciling death now redounds, in the most unexpected places, to those "who love God, who are called according to his purpose" (Rom 8:28).

But more than just claiming that victory, Paul implores his audience not to "be conformed to this *age*" (Rom 12:2, AT) but instead to bear active witness to the age to come. They too are participants in the ongoing cosmic battle against evil; they too are called to the way of the cross, which transforms opposition into reconciling love. Indeed, Paul draws on Jewish tradition as well as Jesus's teachings to offer concrete advice that reflects that way:

Do not repay anyone evil for evil, but take thought for what is noble in the sight of all. If it is possible, so far as it depends on you, live peaceably with all. Beloved, never avenge yourselves, but leave room for the wrath of God; for it is written, "Vengeance is mine, I will repay, says the Lord." No, "if your enemies are hungry, feed them; if they are thirsty, give them something to drink; for by doing this you will heap burning coals on their heads." Do not be overcome by evil, but overcome evil with good. (Rom 12:17–21; see Deut 32:35; Prov 25:21–22)

To live as residents of the messianic age is to bear witness to God's reconciling love even in the face of opposition and evil.

The letter to the Ephesians was written in Paul's name but likely not by Paul himself. In it, the writer further spiritualizes the apocalyptic scenario inherited from the apostle and probably from Jesus as well. For instance, "Paul" writes, that God has "raised us up . . . and seated us with him in the heavenly places" (Eph 2:6). While apocalyptic writers looked forward to positions of glory in the new world order, they didn't insist that they'd *already* attained them.

Likewise, this writer calls Christ "our peace; in his flesh he has made both [Jew and Gentile] into one and has broken down the dividing wall, that is, the hostility between us" (Eph 2:14). All the rancor of Galatians is in a faint speck in the rearview mirror, since the cross has reconciled both groups and eliminated divisive hostility (Eph 2:16). For this writer, the harmony of the messianic age has come to fruition, at least in a spiritual sense.

That's not to say that conflict has disappeared from daily life. Far from it. The writer then has this to say about that conflict:

For our struggle is not against enemies of blood and flesh, but against the rulers, against the authorities, against the cosmic powers of this present darkness, against the spiritual forces of evil in the heavenly places. (Eph 6:12)

The real "enemy" is a spiritual one; the real struggle is against "cosmic powers." But that doesn't make the struggle less real. Indeed, the passage encourages a vigorous fight against evil. It's just that the weapons of war belong to a different world order. They feature an armor of truth, righteousness, peace, faith, salvation, and "the Spirit, which is the word of God" (Eph 2:14–17). This call to arms stirs warriors who wield weaponry that's far more powerful than the most advanced armaments on the market.

The book of Revelation makes a similar point that's often lost on those who tout it as a call to holy war, conventionally understood. Of all New Testament books this is the most apocalyptic in the literary sense; it's an *apocalypsis* ("revelation") to a man named John, who's been banished to an island by imperial forces. And like other Jewish apocalypses from its era, it's riddled with bizarre and violent imagery. The visionary watches as history unfolds toward increasingly devastating ends. Near the end of the vision a rider on a white horse appears who "judges and makes war" (Rev 19:11). This Christlike symbol is tainted with blood and identified specifically as "The Word of God" (Rev 19:13). In the unfolding battle the armies of the earth rise up against him and meet their fate.

But as in Ephesians, the rider bears weapons of a different world order. The sword, we learn, "came from his mouth" (Rev 19:21). Though John's Revelation doesn't downplay the enemies' annihilation, it does suggest that this warrior bears divine power expressly as God's Word. That "Word," or the message embodied in him, easily overwhelms the opposition's force. In the end the visionary spies a "new heaven and a new earth" (Rev 21:1) and hears the promise of the one who is "making all things new" (Rev 21:5). Illuminated by the "glory of God" and the "lamp [who] is the Lamb," Jerusalem becomes once again the center of world peace, as "the kings of the earth bring their glory into it" (Rev 21:23–24).

In all these cases we see evidence that first-century Christians thought they lived in the messianic age. They may have located themselves geographically in the Roman Empire, but spiritually they belonged to a different regime, one that was breaking in to renew the earth. Their challenge was to live as if the cross had set the world free from sin and death even while the forces of evil persisted. It meant seeing God in the most unexpected places; it also meant following the way of inclusive embrace that was setting the whole cosmos to the right.

CONCLUDING THOUGHTS

Does love really win? Did Christ's death really defeat cosmic evil once and for all? Most days it's hard to answer these questions with an unequivocal yes. Perhaps that's why we sometimes look to the cross for little more than a ticket to heaven when we die. But as we've seen, Jesus's earliest followers understood his death in much more grandiose terms. They dared to claim that on the cross God met the forces of concussive violence with a force of reconciling love, and came out with a landslide victory.

What might it mean for his followers today to live *as if* Christ has, indeed, "conquered the world" (John 16:33)? It *doesn't* mean separating his spiritual victory from the realities of our world. It *doesn't* mean glorifying suffering or trivializing it. It *does* mean trusting that God's power is stronger than death, even when death appears to have the upper hand. It does mean, I think, being agents of that power by confronting violence not with more violence but with inclusive love.

It's not as if the power of reconciling love, even in the face of formidable evil, remains entirely hidden from view. As I write, our country has just passed the year anniversary of a tragedy that exposed both cosmic evil and the counter-cultural power of reconciling love. When the Emanuel Nine met their violent fate during a Wednesday evening Bible study in Charleston, most of the country thought evil had carried the day. But just days after the tragedy some family members offered impromptu words of forgiveness, extending the inclusive embrace of God's love even to a troubled young man who had acted as an agent of cold, calculated evil.

True, many have protested this impulsive act of mercy, saying it was too soon, or too easy, or too superficial. But the family members themselves explained that they had no choice. As followers of a crucified Lord, they'd been raised in this way of reconciling love. For them, it was the only way to live as residents of a messianic age in which God's cosmic power of reconciling love reigns triumphant even over the most heinous of evil acts. For them, quite simply, it was the only way to live.

Perhaps the time is right, then, for the church to reclaim the cosmic power of the cross, to live together in ways that affirm, with Teilhard de Chardin, that "the physical structure of the universe is love." Perhaps the time is right to bear active witness to God's power to "conquer and embrace the enemy," as Miroslav Volf writes, not through violence but through reconciling love. Perhaps in this way we will find ourselves set free from the cosmic power of death that looms near, saved from the present evil age through our allegiance to a God who makes "all things new" (Rev 21:5).

Closing Invitation

*Hope's home is at the innermost point
in us, and in all things. It is a quality of
aliveness. It does not come at the end,
as the feeling that results from a happy
outcome. Rather, it lies at the beginning,
as a pulse of truth that sends us forth.*
—CYNTHIA BOURGEAULT,
MYSTICAL HOPE

The cross has a context, and this context leads to Palestine. So much of the story started there, in a tiny little corridor of human history, in a country the size of New Jersey, surrounded by mighty regional powers. So much of the story has continued, across the millennia, as the people of Palestine—Canaanites, Israelites, Jews, Christians, Muslims—have endured one occupation after another. Suffering, humiliation, and oppression have been their daily bread.

The cross has other contexts as well, other places across the globe where successive empires have occupied and divided and despoiled the land. From Korea and Tibet in Asia, to the Ukraine in Eastern Europe, to South Africa and Guatemala and Colombia, our world is just waking up to the horrors of colonialism and its encoded systems of subjugation.

What is unique in Palestine is that this struggle to find meaning in a life full of suffering has been preserved and passed on from one generation to another for thousands of years. This is what we call salvation history—the story that says God is at work to set the world free from suffering and death. It's the story that finds its lifeblood in the hope that "the arc of the moral universe is long, but it bends toward justice."[1]

Within this story one event stands out as a decisive moment of revelation. Somehow, in the crucifixion of their Lord, our ancestors in Palestine were able to find in the midst of suffering a meaning for life. Even more, they were able to find God in the midst of their suffering. In their suffering they were able to spot a "God on the cross" who shared their suffering. This revelation gave them the power not only to endure pain, but also to resist creatively empires and oppression. The revelation of the cross—and its life-giving power—helped them reimagine life in a context marked with death and to find hope in unexpected places. From Palestine this people of the cross went forth with a story to share, good news to proclaim, and a precious hope to kindle. It turns out this was the very hope that the world was waiting for, thirsting for, even dying to find.

This hope is still alive today in Palestine and in many contexts across the world. Hope is not the notion that tomorrow is going to be better; that is mere optimism. Real hope is something different. It lies "at the beginning," wherever the "quality of aliveness" sets us free from the oppressive forces still haunting the human predicament. It's the legacy for all people of the cross, in any place and time, who've been drawn into God's story of salvation.

Let us share a glimpse of hope in the midst of suffering that's dear to us both. In the "little town of Bethlehem" an organization called the Diyar Consortium actively fosters hope and human thriving from "cradle to grave." Started over two

---

[1] This saying is often attributed to Martin Luther King, Jr., who included it in several sermons and speeches. Historians trace it back to the nineteenth-century sermons of a Unitarian minister and abolitionist named Theodore Parker.

decades ago by Christmas Lutheran Church, Diyar provides summer camps, concerts and dance performances, and wellness programs for the aging population. Its crowning jewel, Dar al-Kalima University, offers a robust academic program for students in the arts. There the next generation of painters, travel agents, documentary filmmakers, and chefs refine their skills while learning to think critically as world citizens. Why would Muslim and Christian students sometimes travel hours through several checkpoints just to get to campus? It's because they find there the necessary tools for a life worth living and a community that believes they have something to offer the world. It's there, right under the thumb of daily indignities, that they find hope.

It was this glimpse of hope—and others like it—that Suzanne's family first encountered during a visit to Palestine and Israel over ten years ago. As part of a sabbatical spent learning about Christianity in other cultures, Suzanne, her husband, Bob, and their three children lived for a month at Tantur Ecumenical Institute, right on the border between Jerusalem and Bethlehem. It was during that month that both the cross and the hope it inspires took on new meaning.

For one thing, it was the first time in her forty years that Suzanne had located herself—physically and spiritually— alongside a subjugated people. It was the first time she felt, deep in her belly, the dehumanizing effects of oppression. Just standing in line to cross into Bethlehem brought a nauseating and visceral response to the young Israeli soldiers, who seemed to make a game of treating the Palestinians like cattle.

There were other formative moments. Dar al-Kalima's founding leader, Nuha Khoury, was sharing the school's vision when she was interrupted by a staff person speaking in animated Arabic. Tears filled Nuha's eyes as she related, in English, news that her family's hotel had just been confiscated by Israeli soldiers—less than a week after Israeli courts had recognized the family's rightful ownership. In these and so many other encounters the fact that the Palestinians today are a people on the cross grew hard to ignore.

The good news, though, is that the cross isn't the end of the story. Even in the midst of suffering many Palestinians find a pulsating "quality of aliveness" that's the essence of hope. Suzanne's family saw it at Diyar's day camp, where their children crossed boundaries of language and culture to play badminton and ping pong and soccer with Muslim and Christian children. They saw it, too, in the home of their Muslim taxi driver Samer, who became their personal chauffeur for the month. Gathered around a table with several generations of Bethlehem natives, they shared a meal that can only be called sacramental. It was in this evening of vulnerable solidarity, of self-offering, of recognizing the image of God in one another, that hope came even more powerfully to life.

In this book we've tried to point to the cross as a symbol not of tragedy but of hope, not of death but of life. And while books about the cross and its saving power abound, we hope this one stands out because it's a conversation that crosses boundaries of time and space and culture to bring into clearer view many ways in which Jesus's death continues to liberate us. It's a dialogue between first-century Palestine and the Palestine of today. It's a dialogue between an American and a Palestinian. It's a dialogue between a theologian and a biblical scholar, a woman and a man, and a professor and a pastor. It's a dialogue at a crossroads.

Our world today stands at a crossroads, in dire need of meaningful, life-giving dialogue on a large scale. Oppressive governments inflict suffering on people without listening, really listening, to their voices. Multinational corporations worship the bottom lines with little regard for the well being of their employees. Fundamentalist religious movements exert power through terrorizing tactics that they say their God has prescribed. The cross reminds us where to find God today, and it's in none of these places—not in the allies of power and violence but in the midst of those crushed, marginalized, and silenced. Listening to their cries is what the cross is all about. Joining their struggle, it turns out, is part of the Easter journey to hope. Will you join us?

Index